# WHERE DOGS DWELL

If you pursue justice you will achieve it
and put it on like a festal gown.
Birds consort with their kind,
justice comes home to those who practice it.

—*Ecclesiasticus 27: 8-10*

*May you enjoy reading these stories as much as I enjoyed writing them.*

*Kathleen P. Kelly*
*250-809-5973*

DEDICATED to the women and men worldwide who strive for social justice and human rights.

Agio
PUBLISHING HOUSE

Gabriola, BC Canada V0R 1X4

Copyright © 2022, Kathleen Ann Kelly. All rights reserved. Permission has been obtained for all photos not taken by the author.

Without limiting the rights under copyright reserved above, no part of this publication may be reproduced, stored in or introduced into a retrieval system, or transmitted, in any form or by any means (electronic, mechanical, photocopying, recording or otherwise), without the prior written permission of both the copyright owner and the publisher of this book.

*Where Dogs Dwell*
ISBN 978-1-990335-15-0 paperback
ISBN 978-1-990335-16-7 ebook

Agio Publishing House is a socially responsible enterprise, measuring success on a triple-bottom-line basis.

10 9 8 7 6 5 4 3 2   1f2

# WHERE DOGS DWELL

A nun's solidarity as a nurse midwife
in South America in the
turbulent 1970s and '80s

※ ※ ※

*This memoir is a true story.
Some locations and individuals' names
have been changed to respect their privacy.*

※ ※ ※

Kathleen Ann Kelly

Facing page: *This is a photo of a wool hand-embroidered tapestry made by an Aymara Peruvian woman in the Andes. After having enjoyed it for many years I donated it to the Immigration Center in Fort MacMurray (Northern Alberta). It hangs on the wall for all to love and admire.*

# PART I

## 1972

"Though we travel the world over
to find the beautiful, we must carry it with us
or we will find it not."

—*Ralph Waldo Emerson*

Chapter One

# FROM ENGLAND TO PERÚ

A voice echoed through the nurses' residence in Manchester, England. "Sister Kathleen, there's a call for you on the lobby payphone."

*Who's phoning me this late in the evening?*

From my sitting position in bed, I removed the heavy nursing books from my lap to the dresser before running down the three flights of concrete stairs. In the autumn semi-darkness of the lobby, I picked up the dangling receiver. "Hello, Sister Kathleen speaking."

Through heartrending sobs came the audible words. "I can't go."

It took me several seconds to recognize Sister Ursula's voice. "What do you mean, you can't go? What's wrong?"

"I failed my medical examination." A long pause. "My chest x-ray showed a shadow in the lower lobe of my right lung." She blew her nose before continuing. "They'll take a biopsy later this week."

"Bloody Hell." This wasn't a typical expression for me to use but student nurses said it many times a day. Whenever a nurse said this in front of me, she'd say, "Sorry, Sister." I offered no apology for my visceral response. "This is shocking news, Sister Ursula. How are you feeling?"

"I tire easily but otherwise I'm okay. I wouldn't have known anything was the matter if they hadn't of done the chest x-ray as part of my application for a visa."

"You're young and with treatment you'll heal quickly. Then you'll be able to go to Perú."

I was lying. We both knew she'd never work in the Peruvian Andes at an altitude of 3,400 metres.

Being more realistic and truthful than I, Sister Ursula said, "No, I won't be able to serve God in Perú. He must have other plans for me."

"Perhaps you're right," I mumbled. "He must have other plans for you."

We remained silent for what seemed a very long time. Sister Ursula broke the silence with a question. "Kathleen, would you go to Perú in my place if Mother General agrees? It'd be a consolation to me if you were the sister to replace me. I know you volunteered and Mother General denied your request."

"That's right. Before the volunteers' meeting she told me I was too young. After the meeting she said, 'You are only 25 years of age. You don't have a professional career or perpetual vows or previous missionary experience.' These are her non-negotiable prerequisites."

"Yes, I remember the stipulations. However, since I can't go, she may have to compromise. I'll be devastated if the sister who replaces me isn't yearning to go. You and I have dreamed about being a missionary sister in Perú." She was choking back tears. "It's no longer a reality for me but I want it for you. Would it be okay with you, Sister Kathleen, if I suggest to Mother General that you be my replacement?"

"Okay, you may ask but you know that I'm not a full member of the congregation."

"Yes, I'm aware of this. What you may not know is that Sister Mariana has suggested an experimental community, sisters and laity living together, for the Peruvian mission. We're too small a congregation to spare four sisters. Two lay female teachers have volunteered to go with her. The three of them are prepared to leave within the fortnight."

"Really? How did Mother General respond to this arrangement?"

"Sister Mariana was told that she had to have another sister with her besides the two teachers. That's why I think Mother General may very well let you be my replacement."

"I don't know why I'm attracted to South America; I just am. Perhaps in another lifetime I was Peruvian! Thanks for putting my name forward. I'll keep you in my prayers for the biopsy next week. God willing, Mother General will accept your proposal. Good night and God bless."

※ ※ ※

THE PERUVIAN MISSION OF THE 1970s came in response to Pope John XXIII's plea in the Second Vatican Council to every religious congregation to open a mission in South America.

Within the week, Mother General phoned. "Sister Kathleen, do you still want to go to Perú?"

"Yes, Mother, I'm eager to nurse in Perú." *I'll nurse in the mountains and villages where there are no doctors or hospitals to attend to the sick and dying. I'll bring them comfort and healing.*

"You may replace Sister Ursula in opening the new Peruvian mission," Mother said in her English accent. "Please don't share this until I've announced it to the sisters."

"Thank you, Mother." I was ecstatic. I phoned Sister Ursula. "I'm going to be a missionary sister in Perú!"

"Oh, Kathleen, I'm happy for you. What's the plan now?"

"I can't go right away but I'll graduate as a British registered nurse in early November. The following week I'll fly to Montreal to pronounce Perpetual Vows in my sister Bonnie's parish. My mother will come from Kenya."

"Sounds great. I'll be with you in spirit, Kathleen. When will you leave for Perú?"

"In the early new year. I'll spend Christmas with Mum and the family. And Hogmanay with the sisters in Upstate New York. I'll leave from New York City for Lima in January."

"We'll miss you. Remember to write to us from Perú. In English!" Sister Ursula joked.

"For sure. I'll miss all of you as well. Sister Ursula, I'm grateful to you for opening the door to Perú for me. Your spirit will be with me as I live and work amongst the Peruvian people. ¡*Adios, mi amiga!*"

"*Adios.*"

Sister Mariana packed, and obtained a Peruvian visa, all within two weeks. She seemed indifferent as to whether another sister would be in the experiment community or not. A delay wasn't in her agenda. She was a first-generation Hispanic-American residing in England, and anticipated the celebration of her thirtieth birthday in South America.

After it was announced that I had been chosen to go to Perú, Sister Mariana phoned and said, "Hey, Sister Kathleen, I hear you're replacing Sister Ursula and will be my companion for the new mission. The two teachers and I will leave London for Lima in two days. See you in Perú. *Chou por ahora.*"

"Chou." *Is this how she communicates? Doesn't she want to*

*know when I'll arrive in Perú? Or how I feel about being Sister Ursula's replacement?*

Everything went as planned. I arrived in Montreal and had a reunion with my mother and siblings. The next day the regional superior, Mother Isabel, arrived by train from Upstate New York with Sister Carmen and Sister Barbara to preside at my perpetual vow ceremony. It was wonderful to have them with me.

Mother Isabel said, "Sister Kathleen, enjoy this time with your mother and family. We'll look forward to having you with us for New Year's."

"Thank you, Mother."

Shortly after I brought in the new year with the sisters, plans began to change.

Mother Isabel's deep-set brown eyes shone with authority. "You don't know Sister Mariana like I know her. Have you heard from her since she left England?"

"No."

"Do you know if she arrived in Perú?"

"No." *It's true. I don't know Sister Mariana well. I do know she's artsy and has a free-spirited side which Mother Isabel doesn't seem to appreciate.*

"I'm not booking your flight until you've heard from her," Mother Isabel informed me.

I was in Limbo. Even though I defended Sister Mariana to the sisters, a mouth full of canker sores and restless nights told me I resented Sister Mariana's lack of communication. Throughout this unsettling situation my guitar was my companion and comfort. I snuggled her against my breast. Her strings plucked my heart cords as sadly as the ballads I sang.

It was Sister Carmen who helped me out of this predicament. She attended teacher's training college and mentioned to a sister in a different congregation, "Mother Isabel won't book a flight to

Lima for Sister Kathleen until she hears from Sister Mariana who may or may not be in Perú."

The sister said, "We've a convent in Callao. Callao is the port city in Lima. Our sisters there could meet Sister Kathleen at the airport. She may live in our convent until she connects with Sister Mariana."

"Oh, this is great news. I think Mother Isabel will feel better about booking a flight to Lima for Sister Kathleen knowing your sisters will meet her."

"It'll be easier for Sister Mariana to contact Sister Kathleen if she's in Lima than if she's in the United States."

"Makes sense. Thanks for your help."

Chapter Two

## FROM PERÚ TO CHILE

The Miami-to-Lima plane waited on the tarmac. Aboard the aircraft I weaved my way through the dimly-lit aisle past sleepy passengers until I found seat 26A. I agonized. *Did the baggage handlers have time to unload the two-hour late New York plane and re-load this plane?* The overwhelming thought of losing my Yamaha guitar was too much for me to bear. I was alone without the support of my family, friends or community. My tongue tasted the warm salty tears of fear and abandonment. I leaned my head against the hard porthole glass. Sleep provided a brief escape from the emotional pain of separation from my loved ones and my guitar.

The bright sunshine woke me and I squinted at the stewardess.

"Buenos dias, Hermana. Desea desayuno?" (Would you like breakfast?)

"Sí, por favor."

"Y café?"

"Sí, por favor."

The intrusive nightmare returned as the stewardess's voice faded. *Where is my guitar? Why didn't I bring it on the airplane with me? Why did I carelessly hand it over to the care of baggage handlers?* The barrage of self-accusing questions ceased with the announcement:

"Seats in the upright position. Store handbags under the seat in front of you. Prepare for landing."

The joy I imagined I'd feel on arrival in Lima, was over-shadowed by the nightmare. This was compounded at the Aduana (Customs) window when the officer stamped my Canadian passport and waved me forward to the exit doors. I frowned and extended my hand to receive my passport but another officer came and ushered me through the exit doors. Two sisters in pale-blue veils and matching dresses smiled.

"Bienvenida a Perú, Hermana Catalina."

"I'm Sister Hyacinth and this is Sister Raymond."

"The Customs Officer didn't return my passport."

Sister Hyacinth said, "Asi es la vida aca." (That's life here.)

"We'll go to the immigration office in three days," Sister Raymond assured me. "They'll fingerprint your ten fingers and return your passport."

Fighting back tears I said, "Besides not having my passport I don't have my suitcase or guitar."

"Sister Kathleen, it'll be fine. It's not unusual for baggage not to arrive on the same flight as the passenger. Your suitcase and guitar will be on the later flight from Miami this afternoon and be delivered to the convent. Now let's get you to our convent where you can freshen up and have a nap."

"Thank you, Sister Raymond."

She was correct. After a siesta, I awoke to find my suitcase and guitar alongside the dresser in my room. In a strange way, this reunion with my guitar was symbolic of being reunited with my biological and religious families. It gave me a sense of security in this otherwise unfamiliar environment of people, language and culture.

I was in the country three weeks before Sister Mariana phoned. "Hola, Catalina. Bienvenida a Perú. Que tal?" Her voice thrilled my heart until she said, "Today I enrolled you in the international language school. It's situated in a beautiful area of Lima. It is a four-month course. Classes start next week."

My heart plummeted. "In England we agreed I'd learn Spanish while living with you and the two teachers in the Andes."

"Yes, but the girls think it'd be better for you to learn Spanish in the Lima language school."

Before I could ask, 'Where will I live? How can I communicate with you?' Sister Mariana cut short our conversation. "Bye for now. I've got to go. Talk to you soon. Chou."

"Chou."

My hand put the phone into its holder in slow motion. The dreams and enthusiasm I had for this new experimental community left me. I was limp as a puppet with loose strings. I shared the unwelcomed news with Sister Hyacinth and Sister Raymond.

"Sister Kathleen, know you're not alone," Sister Raymond said. "Together we'll make this strange situation a positive one. I'll go with you to the school. They'll arrange for you to board with a family nearby."

"Most of us really loved being in the language school," Sister Hyacinth comforted me. "I hope it'll be a good experience for you."

"Thanks for your support and encouragement."

Classes were on weekdays between 8:00 a.m. and 12:00 p.m. and from 2:00 p.m. to 4:00 p.m. Lunch was taken quickly to afford us volleyball enthusiasts time for a game between 1 p.m. and 2 p.m. The Peruvian teachers slapped the ball with such force it had us 'gringos' leaping, often landing face first on the court turf.

By the third week of language school, sisters, priests, peace corps volunteers and business workers were united as friends.

In one game, between volleyball slams I spotted Sister Mariana accompanied by a lanky bearded male leaning against the fence. She introduced me to Padre Miguel, her Argentinian priest friend.

"Hola, Catalina. Bienvenida a Perú," he said cheerfully.

"Hola, Padre Miguel."

"Padre Miguel has invited us to form a new experiment community with him in Santiago, Chile," Sister Mariana said excitedly. "The four of us will leave tomorrow. You'll remain here to complete language school, but we'll look forward to you joining us in a few months."

I'm sure my eyebrows arched. I know my mouth opened in a hollow circle. Shocked. "Have you asked permission from Mother General in England to change missions from Perú to Chile?"

She laughed at my naivety and fired back, "I'll inform her once we're set up in Santiago." She left with a lit cigarette held between her shaky fingers.

Sister Mariana wore no veil or other distinguishing religious symbol. Nor did Padre Miguel wear a clerical garb. He dressed in jeans and a bright flowered shirt. *I must look conservative to them in my modified habit: a blue skirt, blouse, veil and small crucifix on a chain around my neck. I need to appear less n-u-n-n-y. It'll be hard enough for me to fit into their experimental community after four months of separation without me arriving dressed like a nun.* To regain perspective, I played Debbie Reynolds's song *Que Sera, Sera* on my guitar. In singing the words I found the courage to persevere in my dream to immerse myself in South America.

When I finished language school, alone and unaware of the political situation in Chile, I took the long bus ride to Santiago. Like Sister Mariana I didn't ask permission of Mother General to leave Perú for Chile. *If I tell her, she'll tell me to return to England. I'm not going to lose this opportunity of being a missionary sister in South America.* We travelled on the dusty highway and from the bus window I saw cotton pickers in the fields and groups of straw houses alongside the fields.

The bus made meal stops every eight hours. The restaurants consisted of high concrete roofs over spacious patios with wooden tables. The menu was fish, rice, salad and a gaseosa (soft drink). The first time I asked, "Por favor, donde esta el bano?" and the fellow pointed outside behind the restaurant, I had my first culture shock. The bathroom was a hole in the ground between two concrete-shaped feet behind a tin wall with an unlatched door. Not easy to target the hole wearing slacks. I soon learned that Chilean women squatted with ease in their wide bright colourful skirts. I whacked away flies as they hovered above the wet ground. *Remember, these flies in their tireless frenzy to survive are playing a ping-pong game between the restaurant and this outhouse. Don't eat or drink no matter what.*

As the bus pulled off the highway for the last restaurant stop on the morning of the fourth day, a male passenger spoke to me in English with a Chilean accent. "Hermana, this is a clean restaurant. They've the best fresh fish sandwich you'll ever taste. Come with me."

The thought of eating a fish sandwich at five in the morning nauseated me, but a sister couldn't show disdain. After all, didn't Jesus eat fish with his apostles? *Hmm,* I had to trust. And to my surprise the fresh fish sandwich was scrumptious.

Sister Mariana, the teachers Selma and Leah, and Padre Miguel met me at the bus depot. We took the local transit. "Los pueblos jovenes are impoverished areas on the outskirts of the city centre," Sister Mariana said. "They're hidden from tourists' view. In the pueblos jovenes people get their drinking water from taps strapped to wooden posts."

"Are you telling me we live in a pueblo joven?"

"Yes. We've built a small wooden house on a corner plot," said Sister Mariana. "It's simple but better than the locals' houses of dirt floors and mud walls."

*Indeed, they've built a simple wooden house; no exaggeration! I sure hope Padre Miguel knows more about his priesthood than he does about building.* The wall separating my bedroom from the teachers' bedroom consisted of crude wooden 2-inch by 6-inch planks stacked horizontally on edge. The planks were warped concave or convex, leaving obvious gaps. My bed consisted of three untreated 2x6 planks supported by two 2x4s screwed to the wall. A mildewed sleeping bag and a thin pillow lay on top. No mattress. I marvelled at the starkness. *I guess this is how the vow of poverty is lived as a missionary.*

Chapter Three

# MY FIRST CHILEAN PATIENT

Sister Mariana asked, "Kathleen, would you please speak with this mother about her children's rash?" before she exited the room. Paola, the 28-year-old mother had five children ranging in age from 8 years to 10 months.

"All my children have this rash," she said. "I could only bring Santitos, Pablito and Marisol with me. The oldest girl, Sarita, is minding el pequinito." I remembered learning in language school that Chileans use the diminutive colloquially: 'ito' for masculine and 'ita' for feminine words.

Earlier in the week a lady had asked me, "Donde vive, Usted?" (Where do you live?)

I understood the question and answered, "Yo vivo en la casa en la esquina," (I live in the house on the corner) as I pointed to it.

She said in a drawn-out voice, "Aw... en la caw si ta en la es skin ita."

I smiled. But inside I screamed *that's what I said in proper Spanish.*

Paola stroked her four-year-old Santitos' head as he snuggled against her oozing breasts while Marisol, the six-year-old, stood shyly behind her mother's chair. Paola's wide colourful woollen skirt and shawl prevented me from observing Marisol's more severe skin condition. *Is this a form of 'machismo' in South American culture? Favoritism of the son, indifference to the daughter?*

Initially, I thought the skin rash was due to not thoroughly rinsing bed linen and clothes. I had watched women hand-rubbing clothes in soapy cold water and rinsing them in an adjacent basin with slightly less soapy water. I knew water was precious and its use restricted by the city from 6:00 a.m. to 6:00 p.m. Neighbours monitored each other. If someone took too much water from the common tap, he or she was scolded by the rest of the neighbours. Paola nodded affirmatively to soap being the possible culprit for the skin condition.

"Instead of washing a bundle of clothes, wash a few at a time," I said. "This way the rinsing water won't be as soapy. I'll get some ointment from the pharmacy to relieve the itching and bring it to your house."

Paola left encouraged after giving me a strong hug. I was happy. *I treated my first Chilean patient. It's rewarding and all I imagined it to be. The joy of showing compassion and care to God's less fortunate.* At 26 years of age, I thought physical poverty, "the poor," represented misery in all its forms. Years later, after having lived with the physically poor, I came to realize they're rich in loving one another, sharing and in cultural values. This realization helped me to shift from materially helping the physically poor to standing with them in their fight for equality and human rights.

When I reached Paola's mud-walled house with the jar of ointment, her two hairless dogs bounded snarling toward me. My heart pounded, my arms were covered in goose bumps, and my tongue cleaved to my jaw (Psalm 137:6). Sarita ordered the dogs to lie down at a distance. I entered the dark windowless house which had stamped earth for flooring. After the cultural hugs were exchanged, I sat on an unstable wooden chair in my white lab coat and asked Paola if the dogs were permitted inside.

"Only at night," she said. "Sometimes they sleep with my children."

*The culprit isn't soap. It's scabies. Dogs with mange transfer their skin disease to people, mostly children, as scabies.* With as much sensitivity as possible I explained, "Paola, maybe the dog's mange is causing the children's skin condition. Perhaps it would be better if the dogs didn't sleep with the children."

Paola was attentive to my medical advice but remained silent. Her warm smile faded, indicating a subtle shift in our trusting patient-nurse relationship. *She's probably worried the skin condition can't be treated since it's not the soap causing the skin rash.*

"Paola, don't worry. I'll bring you some different ointment. The new ointment will clear this skin condition for your children."

Again, she listened but made no comment. I left the house thinking Paola's silence was due to embarrassment. As a sister I was supposed to console not increase worries. From a spiritual perspective I had failed to alleviate Paola's pain. *Jesus console Paola. Help me to show compassion as well as offer medical knowledge.*

The next day, Paola came to our corner house and said to Sister Mariana, "Sister Kathleen offended me. She suggested the dogs shouldn't sleep with my children."

Sister Mariana apologized. "I'll talk with Sister Kathleen. She's new and doesn't know the culture."

After Paola left Sister Mariana called to me, "Kathleen, you can't impose your Western medical training on these locals. The dogs sleep with children to keep them warm at night. June is the beginning of winter in the Southern Hemisphere. The nights will get colder until late October."

"Sister Mariana, I told her the truth and was gentle in saying *maybe* when I knew for certain the cause of the skin condition. If this isn't treated there'll be health complications for her children."

"Yes, I understand. I'll talk with her. But until you learn the culture and are more fluent in street Spanish, it'll be difficult for you to treat the locals."

Sister Mariana's analysis of the situation felt cruel and tears streamed down my face. The exhilaration of the day before was gone. I felt deflated and humiliated.

As a result, I volunteered in the local hospital in order to learn medical terminology, medical ethics and cultural sensitivity. The female surgical unit consisted of six metal military beds with no privacy drapes separating them. Head Nurse Amelia, along with her husband, who was head surgeon, permitted me to work on their unit.

One day I assisted Nurse Amelia's husband in a sternal marrow puncture. I was shocked to see how he laughed and talked with another surgeon who was doing a lumbar puncture in the corner bed. Assuming he was distracted I reminded him, "You haven't given the patient a local anaesthetic."

He smiled. "I'll cause her more pain by giving her a local anaesthetic. Watch. I'll be in and out before an anaesthetic could have effect."

Eyes widen above my cloth surgical mask as I witnessed his professional speed and accuracy. He was correct. My patient appeared more stunned than in pain. As if she had been stung by a wasp.

On another occasion I watched as Chilean nurses and doctors saved a hepatically comatose female patient. "To keep the three-way tube inserted in her trachea at an angle, I'll tie a string to this empty coke bottle and fling it over a bed screen," Nurse Amelia said. "I'll maintain pressure at 0.5mmHg to keep the rubber bubble at the end of the tube inflated. This pressure will prevent further bleeding."

When the patient was stabilized Nurse Amelia explained, "We couldn't insert crushed ice in the bubble as it'd melt too fast."

The hospital wasn't air conditioned. Chilean doctors and nurses had invented an alternative method to save this patient's life. She gained consciousness in a few hours and wanted supper.

Prior to discharge, the doctor sat on the edge of this elderly patient's bed. "Señora, you have to stop drinking. It nearly killed you this time."

Standing on the opposite side of the bed I wondered how many times there had been before this time. The elderly woman leaned forward, took the doctor's hand in hers, and with a twinkle in her beautiful deep brown eyes assured him, "¡No tomo mucho!" (I don't drink much.)

Her charming manner caused both the doctor and I to laugh. He knew that there wasn't any point in lecturing her. Wiser to show her love and acceptance. *This is cultural sensitivity in action. Chilean doctors have a human-medical relationship with their patients.* In that moment I understood my un-attached approach to treating a patient needed to change. I needed to form a friendship before treating a patient and maintain it during and after treatment if I wanted to work successfully in South America.

## Chapter Four

## CHILE

In July 1972 protesters lit bonfires on the main streets of Santiago and food was rationed. I witnessed the demonstrations as I commuted by micro bus daily to and from the hospital. Sometimes the protests were violent and prevented my getting home after work. Because there were no phones in the pueblo joven, I couldn't let Sister Mariana know that I was safe. She had to wait and see if I turned up. Not returning home after work became the norm.

"Who are the protesters? Why are they protesting?" I asked Sister Mariana.

"The wealthy right-wing conservatives raised the price of food. President Salvador Allende and his Marxist government have put a freeze on food prices and on property ownership. The landlords closed all shops in retaliation."

I waited patiently in the street lineup with my ration coupon for quatro pancitos (four bread buns). When it was my turn I handed the server my coupon and he gave me the buns. As I turned to go home, I saw a mother with a toddler on her back and three youngsters holding her skirt. "Señora, here," I said, "take these four bread buns for your children."

As I neared the corner, I heard a raised voice coming from our house. Inside, Selma's hands were flapping in pace with her flapping tongue as she admonished Sister Mariana, "You gave away our oil ration, Sister Mariana. You had no right to do this."

*She'll scream when she hears I gave the bread ration away as well.* I was right. When I tried to explain why I'd given away our bread, she was furious. She turned her anger on me. "YOU, Catalina, can give away YOUR ration but YOU have **no right** to give away MY ration."

I shared a glance with Sister Mariana. She smiled. *I think Sister Mariana and I are more alike than I realized.*

This wasn't the only time Selma admonished us. She ground eggshells into powder and expected us to consume a teaspoonful with our mug of tea, explaining, "You need a daily intake of calcium and there's no milk or cheese now that food is rationed."

*I'll die before I put crushed eggshells into my mouth. I know where they've come from!*

※ ※ ※

THE LOCAL NEWSPAPER SHOWED A cartoon of two Chilean women in a food lineup. The caption below the cartoon read "En que cola vive Usted?" (In what lineup do you live?) The point was not only how much time we spent in obtaining daily food rations, but what were our various needs. Initially, kiosks remained open to sell cigarettes, soft drinks and sweets, but then the sign NO HAY CIGARILLOS hung on closed shutters. Eventually every sign read NO HAY and everyone knew there was nothing of anything to buy.

In the midst of this turmoil my cousin, Charlotte, came to visit me overnight on her South American tour. I went to the airport to meet her. At the arrival door, she smiled broadly, revealing deep-set dimples. We excitedly hugged until her body stiffened in my arms.

"Why are these armed soldiers in the airport? I thought you had a democratically-elected Marxist president who is a physician; not a soldier."

I whispered, "We'll talk later."

The soldiers wore green berets on their egg-shaped heads with a pencil-width of brown hair showing between their berets and ears. They all wore dark-rimmed sunglasses to appear identical. Such uniformity shouted **together we are a formidable force.** In full combat gear they guarded escalators, baggage carousels, exit doors and washrooms.

"Charlotte, I'm glad you have your backpack and handbag with you."

"I travel lightly."

I whisked her to the exit doors before we drew the attention of either the soldiers or the airport personnel. In the warm Chilean sunshine Charlotte relaxed. We pushed away the thick hands of unofficial chauffeurs attempting to grab Char's backpack through the open taxi door. Our official chauffeur was clean shaven, smelled of lavender aftershave, and said, "Wheel… cum… where you go?"

"Gracias, Hotel del Plaza, por favor."

The taxi pulled into dense traffic but our chauffeur was unperturbed by diesel wafting through the open windows or by the incessant honking of horns. He weaved his way effortlessly between automobiles and micros with passengers hanging from the open doors, clinging to one another, sandaled feet on the lowest step, balancing like trapeze artists.

Char squeezed my forearm. "Does anyone ever fall from these micros?"

I shook my head from side to side with closed eyes. *She doesn't need to know I hang from the micro's open door on my daily commute to and from the hospital.*

"Hotel del Plaza... here."

Our driver leaned back to receive the fare and hopefully a tip in American dollars. I didn't disappoint him. The hotel porter opened the back door, pulled the backpack onto a trolley, sending metal-on-metal screeches into the atmosphere. He pushed the wobbly trolley into the hotel entrance and waited for Charlotte and I to enter, hand raised for a tip. I noticed his diminished height and his Down Syndrome facial features. We smiled. I placed an American bill in the palm of his short chubby hand. He left to unload the next taxi.

In Charlotte's hotel room we hugged again. "You need to sleep and I need to do my afternoon shift at the hospital. I'll return later. Perhaps we'll go for a walk in the park before supper."

"That'd be great, I need to move. I've been sitting all day."

"Sleep well, see you later."

When I returned, I found Charlotte in a fetal position in bed, shivering. "What's the matter, Char? Are you sick?"

"No. I was woken by loud shouting in the street. There were bonfires below the window and people throwing telephone books from the hotel onto the fires. Then soldiers dressed in military combat arrived throwing cans which exploded causing a horrible smell and cloudy air and people ran in all directions." Tears of anger and fear crept from Charlotte's narrowed eyes. "How can you live here?" she asked.

Saddened, I said, "Unfortunately, Char, you've arrived at a terrible time. This is one of Chile's worst political moments. It's over for today. Get dressed and we'll go for a walk."

It astounds me now to realize how immune I had become to the violence. Obviously, I had developed a survival technique.

In the lobby doorway Char said, "Will this doorman know if I could buy cigarettes in the hotel?"

"I'll ask him."

He said, "If you would dine in the hotel this evening, perhaps I could bring you some cigarettes."

Once outside I said, "This is supporting black market, Char. Are you aware of this?"

She glared. "Right now, I need a cigarette."

After our walk, we sat in the hotel dining room at a table with an overhanging white tablecloth, a votive candle, and a long-stemmed rose in a slim vase. The waiter leaned forward, slyly dropping a carton of cigarettes in Charlotte's lap from beneath his arm towel as he poured red wine into her glass. She slipped him some money and he wiped the neck of the bottle before slowly retreating. *What a shrewd black marketeer.*

Due to the curfew, I stayed the night with Charlotte. In the morning we hugged and whispered our goodbyes. She left the hotel for the airport and I went to the hospital as usual.

Except nothing **that day** in the hospital was as usual.

Chapter Five

## A SNAPSHOT MEMORY

The front-page headline read **PARO NACIONAL**. A complete shutdown for twenty-four hours organized by the Left Wing. This followed President Salvador Allende's powerful speech on December 5, 1972 when he condemned EEUU (the USA) and called them 'Imperialists'. I didn't comprehend the significance of these words. Nor did I connect them with Nurse Amelia's absence. It felt uncanny and intimidating in the hospital without my translator and colleagues. My spiritual voice assured me. *It's okay, Kathleen, you can show compassion and empathy without a fluency in Spanish.* I focused on my patients and completed my shift.

The next day Nurse Amelia and staff were in the hospital when I arrived.

"Good morning, Nurse Amelia."

She ignored me and completed patients' rounds with the surgeons. Normally Amelia translated if she thought I didn't understand what the patient said. Today she offered no translations. For the rest of the morning, she stayed in her office. *Perhaps Amelia has a migraine, or a bad menstrual period.* At lunch hour Amelia went to the cafeteria without me.

When I placed my tray on her table, she and her two nurse friends took their trays to another table leaving me alone. I froze.

After lunch I stood in Amelia's office doorway. "Why did the three of you walk away when I came to the table?"

She answered in rapid Spanish.

Confused, I asked, "Why are you speaking to me in Spanish when I can't understand what you're saying?"

She spoke louder and more aggressively.

"Why are you treating me this way?" I asked, my voice quivering. "Tell me, Amelia, what's wrong?"

She walked defiantly towards me. When she was inches in front of my face, she shouted in English, "WHO ARE YOU?"

"You know who I am. I'm a sister, a British trained nurse, and I'm Canadian."

She roared, "YOU ARE C.I.A."

This is a snapshot memory for me. Examples of snapshot memories in our time: JFK's killing, Princess Diana's fatal car accident, Nine-Eleven. A person will always remember exactly where they were when these events occurred. I know I was in Amelia's office doorway when I first heard the designation C.I.A.

"You're a right-wing supporter like all Catholics," Amelia continued.

"I'm not political, Nurse Amelia. I don't support any wing."

"Why did you work yesterday?"

"Because I'm a nurse and there were patients who needed help."

She grunted, "Basta!" through clinched jaws, neck veins bulging and fanned-out fingers in front of her face. She stomped across the floor tiles to her metal desk. "VAYA DE AQUI." (GET OUT OF HERE!)

I stood immobilized in the doorway with the initials C.I.A. hanging in the air until my shaking legs carried me down the wide smooth grey concrete stairs onto the crowded street of protesters. Sweat rolled from my armpits over the ribs of my trembling body. My hair was damp with perspiration. Derogatory slogans crackled from loudspeakers on the back of pick-up trucks. *"Foreigners out of Chile... forty-eight hours."*

I was petrified and feared for my life. *It doesn't matter that I'm Canadian. I'm white. In their eyes I'm North American and therefore the enemy.* It was too dangerous for me as a redheaded blue-eyed gringa to remain on the streets. I looked for somewhere to hide. Before I could find a place, I was shoved by a passerby and tumbled down a slope to land behind a toppled billboard. To this day, I have no idea how I made it home to our experimental community. I don't know if I returned the same day or several days later.

The next memory I have is of Sister Mariana, Padre Miguel, Selma, Leah and myself sitting round the wooden table staring silently into the darkness, listening to the loudspeakers' repeated slogan: *"Foreigners out of the country... forty-eight hours"* until the early hours of the morning. We huddled in blankets, discussing plans over a bottle of Chilean wine. Who would stay? Who would leave? What were our options?

"We've decided that it'd be best for you to leave Chile, Catalina," Padre Miguel said. "You're politically naive, lack fluent Spanish, and appear North American." *Yeah, as opposed to your Hispanic/Argentinian features.* "We four are going underground. We will make our way to my home in Argentina."

"Let me stay with you," I begged.

"Catalina," Sister Mariana said in a calm voice. "I don't want you to have a nervous breakdown when President Allende's government is overthrown. President Nixon, as others before him, is plotting to instigate a coup to overthrow President Allende's government. When Allende nationalized the copper industry it escalated their determination to oust him. It was for this reason Nurse Amelia accused you of being C.I.A. The Central Intelligence Agency provides information to the United States government about politics in non-American countries. That's why you must leave." I stared at her in disbelief. "It'll be a brutal time in Chile when the overthrow happens," she continued. "We hope we'll be in Argentina when it does."

Leah offered me more wine. I nodded.

Sister Mariana continued, "You're 26 years of age and have a future. I want you to leave tomorrow evening for your own safety, Kathleen. Miguel and I will accompany you in a taxi onto the airport grounds. The taxi driver is a friend of ours. He'll drop you at the airport and bring us home."

The decision was made. I was a threat to the group's survival.

Armed soldiers lined roads leading to the airport and thronged inside. They hurried us foreigners through customs barely checking our passports. It was evident they wanted us out of Chile NOW. My body shook. My eyes were so wide open I thought they'd never close again. My mouth was dry. In the boarding terminal washroom, abdominal cramps provoked a two-way sensation of wanting to vomit and to empty my bowel. Standing with my foot on the ceramic toilet bowl, I could do neither. I wailed loudly. *I've longed to be in South America. I don't want to live anywhere but here.* Between sobs I heard: "Foreigners board the plane to Miami, Florida. AHORA."

I sank into the window seat and moaned again. *I've longed to be in South America. I don't want to live anywhere but here.*

We took off and fifteen minutes later touched down in Lima's Jorge Chavez airport en route to Miami, where my cousin Charlotte boarded the aircraft.

"Oh, Kathleen, I'm so relieved to see you." She sat beside me and held me in her arms.

As the airplane lifted upwards, I stared at the South American soil disappearing beneath night clouds. With a broken heart I made a vow, *I'll return to South America and when I do, I'll have a strong political stance. I'll never again be expelled because I don't understand the political situation or am naïve about oppression. I'll be a religious advocate for the poor against corrupt politics no matter whether the corrupt politics are internal or external.*

Inside Miami airport, on the down escalator we had a panoramic view of passengers returning from somewhere or waiting to leave. I saw flamboyantly-dressed men and women in large straw hats, Bermuda shorts, brightly-coloured shirts. The shirts were unbuttoned due to expanded girth. The people spoke and laughed loudly. I was ashamed to be white and of the same culture.

My cousin Paulette, Charlotte's sister, and her husband, Eric, met us in the arrivals lounge. They knew nothing of the rations in Chile nor of the over-throw of Allende's government. The realities of Miami and Chile were bi-polar, yet only six flying hours apart.

"Let's go to a restaurant before heading home," suggested Eric. "You girls must be dying to have all-American food."

The plates around us contained as much food as would feed a Chilean family. I literally couldn't eat on seeing the abundance. When Eric noticed I hadn't touched anything on my plate he cheerfully said, "We'll ask for a doggie bag." My face must have shown horror. He explained, "Kathleen, it's a polite way of saying we'll barbeque this food tomorrow."

When Eric asked, "What do you love about the South American culture?" I passionately replied, "I met *real* people."

He laughed. "Are we not real people, Kathleen?"

"NO. The people there are *real*."

I was unfamiliar then with Carl Jung's description of the persona (the false self). How people often hide behind a mask that gives them the appearance of who they think they ought to be. In Chile, people lived without a mask and intuitively I knew the difference.

I had had my own experience in Chile of living without a mask. I was baking and my apron had flour on it and my sleeves were rolled up but I had to go to the kiosk for an egg.

Initially I was frustrated with the inconvenience of having to change my clothes before leaving the house. Then I realized *I can walk to the kiosk without removing my apron or rolling down my sleeves. I can go as I am without anyone looking sideways at me.* It was liberating. The reality was I was baking. I didn't have to remove the apron, roll down my sleeves, comb my hair or pretend. Pretend what? That I wasn't baking? I learned that in poverty there's no pretense. The wealth of poverty is the freedom to be ***real.***

# PART II

## TEN YEARS EARLIER

## Chapter Six

## The Funeral

Relatives and friends paused in front of my father's photo. Some tearful, some pensive, yet together in grief, they processed into the dimly-lit funeral parlour. They offered condolences to my mother, to my three siblings, and to me before edging their way to the coffin. Aunt Miriam stared wide-eyed at her brother in the mahogany satin-lined box. She gazed at Ted's dead white face against his silvery black hair. She cried and giggled behind her gloved hand. Bewildered.

Aunt Miriam approached Mother. I overheard their hushed conversation. "Ona, I tell you, Ted is better dressed now than he was in life."

Leona, my mother, raised her eyebrows and rolled her eyes. "Yes, that's because he's laid out in a friend's suit."

"What?" Aunt Miriam blurted out.

My mother, embarrassed by some guests' raised eyebrows, guided her into an alcove. "Ted and I had an invitation to a wedding next week. Ted told his friend, Ken, that he wouldn't go because he didn't have a suit. Ken offered him a loan of his dressy suit. That's Ken's suit you're seeing Ted in over there."

Aunt Miriam snorted.

Mother continued, "I was in such a state when the undertaker came with the body bag, I didn't notice he had Ken's suit over his arm. I focused on my poor Ted being stuffed…."

Aunt Miriam doubled over with laughter. "Ona, stop it… my sides are going to burst."

But the memory brought a fresh bout of sobbing for my mother. I watched Aunt Miriam and Mother rock back and forth in a tearful embrace.

When the parlour was empty, I stood beside my father's coffin. I remembered how he'd sing the Irish ballad *I'll Take You Home Again, Kathleen* when I was a little girl. "One day, Kathleen, you and I will go to Ireland," he'd tell me. At four years of age, I didn't know how far Ireland was from Montreal. It didn't matter. My father was a dreamer. I understood the importance wasn't the dream but the ability to dream.

My mother was a realist. She'd say, "Ted, why are you telling this child your pipedreams? We don't have two cents to rub together." *Why does she always have to ruin our time together with her words?*

Alone in the funeral parlour with Dad I heard, *"Live our dream, Kathleen, go to Ireland."*

"I will." I promised.

Lost in the imagery of Ireland's green fields and wind blowing my hair I felt a gentle caress. Turning, I buried my wet face in my best friend Isaac's chest.

"Kathleen, let's go to White's." White's was the teen hangout restaurant two blocks from the funeral parlour.

"Yeah, let's go. I need to get out of here. And I need to tell you something."

"What?"

"Just wait."

We walked the two blocks hand in hand. It felt good to hold Isaac's hand. It was soft and warm. I felt like a normal teenager again. In the funeral parlour, the old people had all been dressed in black. Their solemn faces depressed me. In the restaurant Isaac and I squeezed into a corner booth. From the window we watched the low sun set between the houses and city traffic.

"So, what do you want to tell me, Kathleen?"

"My mother is moving the family after the burial," I said. "My father signed the rental agreement, not my mother. With Dad gone the rental agreement is no longer valid."

"Are you going to end up on the street?"

"No. We're moving to Ville St. Laurent where I'll go to a private school with my cousins."

Isaac raised his head from sipping soft ice cream through a straw. "I hope you won't become a snob! Can we still be friends?"

"Of course, we'll always be friends, Isaac. Let's get back to the funeral parlour before my mother notices I left."

"Yeah, okay."

My mother was readying herself to leave with some relatives. I left with them. Within a week, we had a funeral, a burial and moved. There was no time to grieve. Grief went underground. It didn't resurface for three decades, until I was forty-two years old. My coping strategy at fifteen for dealing with my father's fatal heart attack was to immerse myself in school activities and teenage life.

The principal in the new school, Mother Aloysius, glanced at my failed eighth-grade report card. "Oh, dear!" she said as she lowered the card onto the table behind her. Then she smiled. "Kathleen, I'm placing you in ninth grade on a three-month trial. If your grades are good, you'll remain in ninth grade. If they aren't, you'll repeat grade eight. Are you in agreement?"

"Yes," I said. *I can't believe that she's doing this for me.*

*I've gotten a new start. I'll run with this football and make a touch-down!*

The ninth-grade students accepted me as an intelligent wealthy classmate in their private school not knowing I came from an impoverished sector of Montreal with a failed report card. My first friend was Irene, who asked, "Where did you go to school last year?"

Embarrassed. I simply said, "I was with French-Canadian sisters in the East sector."

"Why did you move here?

"My father died and my aunt lives here. My mother thought it'd be good if I went to the same school as my cousin, Diane."

"Diane Reardon is your cousin?" Irene exclaimed. "She's such a great figure skater and athlete."

"Yeah," I said proudly.

"Did you like going to school with French-Canadian sisters?

"No, to be honest, I hated them. They were rigid and cruel." I anticipated her next question. "They made us stand in the school yard in military lines under the hot June sun until there was absolute silence. If there was a whisper or a giggle we stood longer. It was torture for me as a redhead. The sisters stood in the shade of the overhanging veranda while we baked."

"Unbelievable," she said. "I see why you hated them! Our American sisters in this school talk to us in the schoolyard and hallways, and even skate with us after school. There's no silence anywhere except in the classroom. Gee, I'm glad you moved here."

"Me too."

"Sorry you lost your father though."

"Yeah, thanks, Irene." After a pause I added, "It's kind of funny because I wanted to be a sister before that experience with those nuns."

"Maybe you'll think of it again when you see how wonderful our American sisters are here."

"Perhaps. Catch you up tomorrow, Irene."

"Okay, so long."

I observed the American sisters for two years. They were happy energetic women. On graduation night I told Mother Aloysius, my siblings and friends that I was entering a missionary order. "It's an order of sisters in Upstate New York. I enter this September."

"I'm not surprised you want to be a sister, Kathleen," Mother Aloysius said. "But I'm sorry you haven't chosen our congregation."

"It's because I want to be a missionary."

Friends said things like: You'll never last. You talk too much to keep silence. You'll miss dancing too much.

My sister, Bonnie, was more affirmative. She said, "Oh, Kathleen, I can see you as a nun and nurse in some faraway country. It suits you."

My brother Anthony said, "Why do you want to throw away your life? Why do you want to dress like a penguin?"

Before I could answer his questions, my mother intervened. "Enough with your rude comments, Tony. You chose the way you live your life. Kathleen chooses the way she wants to live her life."

My mother knew that I had been corresponding with the missionary sisters for the past year. They sent me their quarterly magazine. I devoured articles about sisters', priests' and brothers' work in Asia, India and Africa. I couldn't wait to join them.

"For tonight," said my mother tactfully to everyone, "let's celebrate Kathleen's graduation. You'll have all summer to get used to her decision."

Chapter Seven

## ENTRANCE DAY

On a beautiful autumn day in 1964 Mum and I boarded the train from Montreal to Upstate New York. At times my thoughts went faster than the train. One moment I was certain, the next uncertain. *Am I ready to leave my mother, friends and country? Can I live without dances?*

My mother sensed my anxiety. "Let's walk to the diner car. We'll grab a light lunch."

"Alright."

Thirty minutes later a sister in a black habit and characteristic Franciscan cord waved at us from the platform. *An Audrey Hepburn replica. Just like Audrey Hepburn in The Nun's Story.* The sister took my trunk. "Welcome to the United States. I'm Sister Carmen. You must be Kathleen."

"Yes, thank you, Sister."

"And you, Kathleen's mother?"

"That's correct. I'm Leona."

"Pleased to meet you. Did you have a pleasant trip?"

"Oh, yes, it was lovely," Mother said.

"Sister Barbara is in the minivan. Come this way," Sister Carmen motioned.

The blue minivan had bold lettering FRANCISCAN SISTERS on the sliding door.

"Hi, welcome. I'm Sister Barbara, your chauffeur! Climb in."

"The novitiate house is a farmhouse, typical New England architecture with a wrap-around veranda," said Sister Carmen. "We have a cat and a Siberian Husky, Ruffice. He stays outside."

In panic, I blurted out, "Oh, no, I'm afraid of cats. There *can't* be a cat!"

Sister Barbara pulled the van off the road. Looked straight at me through her rimless glasses, and said, "We've had Mittens ten years. She stays; *you* decide if you can live with her."

I didn't know whether to laugh or cry. I repeated in a softer tone, "I'm afraid of cats."

The drive resumed. Sister Carmen spoke as if nothing had happened. "Kathleen, two other 18-year-olds like yourself will become postulants with you tomorrow. At which time you'll meet our novices. For tonight you and your mother may relax in the guest house. Mother Immaculata will be your novice mistress. Once you've settled-in she will come to chat with you."

"Thank you, Sister Carmen," I said timidly.

The next morning Rebecca, Samantha and I knelt on prie-dieus in the small wood-panelled chapel as Mother Immaculata placed a black soft lacy veil on our heads and Sister Carmen tied a black elbow-length cape around our shoulders. A closing hymn was sung. All clapped as we left the chapel.

Outside in the September sunshine my mother hugged me and said, "You look beautiful, Kathleen. I'm happy for you."

"Oh, Mum, I can't believe I'm here. I longed for this day. Thanks for being with me."

*Photo of Rebecca in front of the barns taken on our Entrance Day, September 8, 1964. I have no photo of Samantha who entered with us on this date.*

"Let's have a group photo of the three postulants," Mother Immaculata said with an affectionate smile.

After the group photo I saw Sister Barbara cuddling Mittens. I cringed as she headed towards me.

"Don't worry. Mittens is declawed," she said.

I petted Mitten's calico head and heard her purr.

"Not bad, EH?" Sister Barbara made me laugh with her exaggerated use of EH.

"What part of Canada are you from, Sister Barbara?" I asked.

"I hail from Ontario. Oh, time to eat! Take a plate and serve

*"Can't believe I'm really here entering a convent but am very happy that I'm doing it."*

yourself, Kathleen. You can sit anywhere. Where's your mother? Oh, there she is under the sugar maple talking with Rebecca's parents. Why don't you join them?"

"Yes, okay. Thank you, Sister Barbara."

Rebecca looked more attractive in her black postulant outfit than she did in her secular clothes. Her black curly shoulder-length hair sparkled against the black veil.

"Do you feel as weird as I do in this black outfit?" she said.

"Yeah. And I'd like to exchange these granny shoes for stiletto heels," I responded.

"You're not kidding. And how about a shorter skirt? My legs are trapped at the calves."

We laughed like friends with an akin mischievous spirit. Both of us were shorter than Samantha who was five-foot-six. Her straight posture seemed even straighter as she wore her postulant skirt, blouse, and veil like a military uniform.

Mother Immaculata waited for a lull in the chatter. "It's 4:30 now," she said. "At 5:00 we pray Vespers from the Divine Office prayer book. I invite you to pray with us. After Vespers, postulants and parents may say their goodbyes. Leona, Sister Barbara will take you to the train station."

"Thank you, Mother."

The thought of my mother taking the train without me caused a lump in my throat. I fought back tears while the sisters chanted the Divine Office. Following Vespers, the dreaded moment for postulants and parents arrived. After long embraces and promises to write, we three postulants lowered our heads to hide our tears and walked into the house without looking back.

Sister Paul Ann (assigned as my buddy novice) pulled my trunk to the postulants' dormitory. "Kathleen, it gets better every day. You're not alone. All of us feel homesick at times. We support one another with a smile during 'hours of silence'. Just give me a wink if you think I'm having a rough day and I'll do the same for you. Deal?"

"Deal."

Sister Paul Ann opened the dormitory door. "Here's your cell."

"A cell? This isn't a prison. Is it?" I asked.

"Of course not. Cell is the traditional name used in religious and monastic life for a cubicle. I think it's called a cell to remind us that we aren't to get attached to a place."

I relaxed with this explanation and said, "Okay."

The cell Sister Paul Ann introduced me to was the first in a dormitory of four cells. Each had a single bed, a chair, and a bedside locker. "The curtains are tied back in the daytime and drawn around your bed at night. Every night before Compline, fill this basin—" she pulled it from the shelf in the tin locker, "—with water from the bathroom for your morning wash. There'll be a morning bell to wake you. As soon as you hear the bell, kneel and kiss the floor. A novice will intone the prayer. Keep this typed prayer on your locker until you can recite it by memory. After you've washed and dressed, go empty your basin in the bathroom sink. Dry it and place it back on the shelf. Then draw the curtains back and tie them with the attached strings. Then proceed to the chapel for Matins. Now, follow me." She walked quickly. I heard her habit swish, her wooden rosary beads hanging from her Franciscan cord clicking together as I followed her up a narrow creaky wooden staircase. "Your trunk is kept up here in the attic. You're never to come up here unless you've asked permission from Mother Immaculata. Let's get to the refectory, Kathleen, before we're late and have to ask for a penance."

I knew that Compline was Night Psalms of Forgiveness and Peace before sleep and Matins was Morning Psalms of Praise at the start of a new day, but I didn't know what she meant by "ask for a penance."

After supper one novice after another knelt before Mother Immaculata. The novice mumbled something, kissed the floor and got up. *This must be asking for a penance. Strange.* Rebecca, Samantha and I entered the queue. When I knelt before Mother, she made a sign of the cross on my forehead. It was comforting.

We gathered in the conference/recreation room upstairs. Mother Immaculata welcomed us postulants and told us, "Today is the feast of Our Lady. It's a recreational day; no silence is observed. Tomorrow silence (only whispering permitted) is observed all day apart from the recreational hour after lunch and in the evening before Compline. After Compline, Grand Silence (no whispering) is observed until Matins is prayed at 7:00 a.m. Gradually, silence will become not a lack of talking but a listening to God talking to you." Mother stood and left the room.

The novices resumed their chatter.

*Mother is human yet spiritual in the way she speaks to us. She has a non-threatening, non-judgemental approach. She glides in her habit as would a ballerina. I admire her and aspire to be like her. She doesn't fit the stereotypical image I had of a novice mistress. She is not a stern disciplinarian.*

"Hope you three are baseball players," a novice said. "We play baseball during afternoon recreation when the weather is good."

At 9:00 p.m. the chatter ended. We processed to chapel for Compline. Following Compline, back in my cell with curtains drawn, the tears flowed. I missed my mother. I lay down and buried my head in the wet pillow. I hoped those in the adjacent cells didn't hear me crying.

Chapter Eight

## POSTULANCY

There was nowhere to hide. I assumed that if I kept my hands hidden under my postulant cape, lowered my eyes, walked slowly and bowed when necessary, I'd merit the perfect postulant award! My delusion was shattered when Mother Immaculata summoned me to her office. She recognized my inferiority complex and challenged it. "Kathleen, every time you're presented with a new task you say, 'Oh, I can't do that.' I want you to remember you have entered the American novitiate. The last four letters of the word American are i-c-a-n. From now on I want you to prove to me you can't do something before I hear you say I can't do that."

"Yes, Mother."

She smiled. "You may go now."

"Thank you, Mother."

I came away with a knotted stomach. I quickly learned I couldn't hide my lack of confidence behind my religious garb.

In our spiritual conference, Mother said, "Your postulancy is a time to grow in self-awareness and newness. I expect you to learn to chant prayers in Latin, type, do hand embroidery and ceramics.

I also expect you to attend scripture classes and learn a musical instrument. Learning to build community through prayer, work and recreation, is the ultimate goal."

I took Mother's expectations seriously. I sat at a hard, unpolished wooden desk in the damp unfinished concrete basement and learned from a book to type on a Remington Standard typewriter with no letters on the keys. In this basement postulants and novices spent many hours in contemplative silence, typing, studying… and folding laundry.

Every Saturday morning large wicker baskets of dirty laundry from a nearby seminary were dropped off at the basement doors set into the ground. Two second-year novices lifted the heavy wooden doors and carried the baskets down the uneven concrete stairs into the basement. They laid the baskets beside the wringer washing machine. Sister George, another second-year novice, was in charge of the laundry. As each basket-load of dirty laundry was washed, I'd hear her whisper, "Rebecca and Kathleen, could you please hang these on the clothes lines near the barn?"

"Thank you, Sister," whispered Rebecca.

This provided Rebecca and me the opportunity of chit-chatting while hanging the clothes in the field. I looked forward to this Saturday morning time with Rebecca when we'd exchange our war stories from the past week. Except one Saturday my focus wasn't on what had happened during the week but rather on what hadn't happened. I was in a foul mood.

"Rebecca, doesn't the routine of every day, every week bother you?" I asked.

"No, why? Does it bother you, Kathleen?"

"Yes. I used to look forward to Friday and Saturday for dancing. Now Saturday is for washing men's dirty laundry. Maybe I don't belong here."

"I don't know. Why don't you talk with Mother?"

"Maybe." I knew I didn't need to talk with Mother. I knew why I was in a foul mood: I hadn't had enough sleep. And why didn't I get enough sleep? Because I had leaned out the window alongside my bed until 1:30 a.m. watching young folk from Ricky's Lounge across the dirt road drag racing. The music was loud. My fingers and toes tapped with the beat. I had had four hours of sleep when the morning bell rang at 5:30 a.m. calling us to prayer.

Sister George whispered to me, "You need to learn how to make starch in a deep bucket. Let's get started. Keep stirring, while I pour the boiling water. If you don't stir this gooey grey liquid in unison with my pouring, dumplings will result instead of clear white liquid starch."

Perplexed, I whispered, "Do dumplings happen often?"

"They sure do, honey," Sister George replied in her Southern drawl. "But not if you keep stirring." When we finished making starch, she whispered, "Now you need to learn how to iron wet starched linen. The trick is to run a very hot iron over the linen before the linen knows what hit it! This'll prevent the starch from sticking to the iron or having bubbles form between the layers."

A starched linen band was worn across the forehead under the veil as part of the religious habit. Nearly every Saturday a postulant or novice suffered one of three mishaps: dumplings in the starch, starch stuck to the iron, or bubbles between layers. Each of these had consequences. If dumplings formed, the bucket of liquid starch had to be thrown out and the process started again. If starch stuck to the iron the iron couldn't be used until it had cooled and had been scraped. Two irons were heated alternately on the furnace surface. If we were reduced to one iron it meant an extra laundry day. Still, the most humiliating mishaps of all was creating a bubble! The sister whose band bubbled had to wear it for the week looking like she had a goose egg on her forehead.

Some handled these mishaps better than others. When anything happened to Samantha a tantrum resulted. This caused Rebecca and I to roll our eyes and clear our throats while Sister George consoled, "It's okay, Sam." After supper, Sister George had to ask a penance of Mother for breaking silence.

Mother Immaculata often smiled during Saturday evening penance. No doubt she was reminiscing about her days in the laundry before she went to Borneo for twenty years.

"Asking for a penance teaches self-discipline and humility," she taught us. Even though I valued Mother's explanation, my outward behaviour didn't demonstrate this to my novice mistress. When I knelt before her to ask for a penance I always smiled or giggled. After three consecutive evenings of this behaviour Mother Immaculata said, "Kathleen, since you find this spiritual exercise funny, you'll no longer ask for a penance. Instead, you'll stand beside me while your sisters ask for their penances."

"Yes, Mother," I said uncomfortably.

Not asking for a penance proved to be my penance. The heat from my rosy cheeks brought tears to my eyes whenever Sisters Paul Ann, Barbara or Carmen knelt before Mother Immaculata and me. It was a humiliating experience.

This embarrassing situation ended when Mother Isabel, the regional superior, addressed the community. "On November 21, 1964, Our Holy Father, Pope Paul VI, released his encyclical Lumen Gentium (Light of the Nations). In his encyclical he reminds the faithful of their vocation to follow Christ. He emphasizes that both laity and religious have the same vocation to follow Christ." She paused and took a deep breath. "In the Old Testament it's written, 'I don't want your sacrifice… I want your love.' (Hosea 6:6) and in the New Testament Jesus said, 'I desire mercy not sacrifice…' (Matthew 12:7) Mother General in England recommends the spiritual practice of asking for a penance be suspended. We need to be more diligent in loving Christ than observing religious practices."

Mother Immaculata nodded in agreement.

Mother Isabel went on. "The Second Vatican Council is in process. I anticipate the synod of bishops attending the council will ask us sisters to simplify our lifestyle and be closer to God's people." Mother rose from her seat at the head of the table. "I'll keep you informed of any other changes. May God bless each of you."

"God reward you, Mother," we postulants and novices said reverently. In the convent "God reward you" replaced "thank you."

Mother Immaculata accompanied Mother Isabel out of the room. *This is great. I no longer have to stand beside Mother and watch my sisters ask for a penance.*

※ ※ ※

THE MONTH OF DECEMBER WAS fast upon us. Rebecca, Samantha and I had the leading roles in the play *Little Women* which was performed for Mother Immaculata's feast day on December the 8th. A sister's feast day is the day her religious name is celebrated. A sister's religious name is either in honour of a saint or in honour of Mary. Only after the Second Vatican Council did sisters have the option to reclaim their baptismal name.

"Kathleen, since you've auburn red hair you'll play Jo's character," Sister Carmen said.

"Thank you, Sister Carmen."

"Rebecca, you'll play Meg's character, the calm level-headed sister."

"Thank you, Sister Carmen."

Because Samantha's regular tantrums irritated me, I had an uncharitable thought when Sister Carmen handed her the script for Beth's character: *Yep, she'll imitate Beth's resentment with no effort. And her character dies!*

I was given two long auburn braids to pin under my postulant veil to rehearse Jo's character. In *Little Women,* Jo sells her braids to pay for her father's hospital expenses. Unbeknownst to Mother Immaculata, one morning I wore the braids to Mass. During the homily I casually flung a braid over my shoulder causing Rebecca to snicker and the priest to lose his concentration.

After Mass, Mother shook her finger at me. "No more of your impish behaviour, Kathleen."

"No, Mother."

The Liturgical season of Lent arrived. *I'll be kinder to Samantha. I'll sit beside her at evening recreation instead of avoiding her.* This was my personal Lenten sacrifice which resulted in Samantha and I becoming friends. The communal Lenten sacrifice was no mail for forty days. By Easter Sunday I had accepted that my teenage life of dances was over. I was ready to become a novice. Would Mother Immaculata agree?

Chapter Nine

## THE CANONICAL YEAR

Rebecca, Samantha and I became first-year novices on May 31, 1965. We donned the Franciscan habit, held lighted candles and proceeded up the chapel aisle. Mother Immaculata played *Veni Creator Espiritu* on the organ and the second-year novices sang the lyrics in Latin.

*Wow, God has chosen ME to have a special bond with HIM. God loves ME. Nothing else matters.*

Within the week this *special bond* was challenged when I asked Mother if I might paint the kitchen. "Actually," she said, "the kitchen does look drab. We have a gallon of green paint. No other colour." I noticed how Mother automatically said *'we have'* and not *'I have'*. In the convent, in the sixties, no one personally owned anything. *'I'* became *'we'*.

"Green will look nice with the white fridge and stove. I'll trim the door and window frames white if you'd like, Mother."

"Okay. You may get started," she said with a kindly smile.

I buttoned my floor-length habit up to my waist and tied on an old blue apron. I felt confident about painting and liked the immediate results. But on the third day of painting my elbow struck the can of paint on top of the ladder. A Niagara Falls of green paint streamed down the fridge and stove before splattering onto the black-and-white-checkered linoleum floor.

Mother called down the staircase, "Are you okay, Sister Kathleen?"

I remained silent.

At that very moment a postulant entered the kitchen. Helen was from a wealthy upper-class family and swaggered around with a condescending air. Viewing the disaster, she exhaled. "What happened?"

I flashed my fiery eyes at her and said, "What the hell do you think happened?"

Stunned with my reaction, she kept walking without another question or comment.

I turned and there was Mother Immaculata standing in the corner of the kitchen. She had heard my swearing response. *This kind of behaviour from a novice, even a week-old novice, probably merits an automatic dismissal.* Mother Immaculata beckoned two novices to bring newspaper and clean up the slime.

"Sister Kathleen, come to the refectory."

Once there she poured me a glass of Coca-Cola and said, "As soon as you finish your drink, come to the laundry."

I sipped my drink and wondered what kind of reprimand to expect. I walked slowly to the laundry. There she sat on a chair waiting for me.

"Send me home," I said. "I know I deserve it. Everything I do I ruin." Sobbing, I blurted out one statement after another.

Mother waited for my tirade to finish before saying, "Sister Kathleen, I'm not sending you home. If you want to leave, it's your choice, not mine. Now, let's remove some paint from your clothes. You may shower, put your Sunday habit on, and put this habit in the washing machine. I suggest you ask God to help you to stop berating yourself."

She left the laundry and never mentioned the incident again. I finished painting the kitchen after another gallon of paint was purchased.

※ ※ ※

SATURDAY WASN'T ONLY LAUNDRY DAY it was also our shower day. Novices were expected to be in their clean linen (white veil, linen band, Franciscan cord and Sunday habit) for First Sunday Vespers at 5:00 p.m. One Saturday as I walked towards the chapel in my clean linen, Mother Immaculata motioned me to follow her to the guest parlour.

I frowned. *Am I being sent home?*

At the parlour door Mother read my worried expression and said, "I know Canon Law (church law) says a novice in her canonical year can't have a family visit. I'm treating this as an exception. Your mother has come a long way to speak with you. You may have a half-hour visit with her. You won't have to re-commence your canonical year. Go ahead."

When I opened the door and saw my smiling mother, joy welled up in my heart. After a long warm embrace, we sat on the sofa clasping hands.

"I've written to you about my voluntary work on the Northern Reserve in Ontario," she said.

"Yes, I've enjoyed your letters, Mum. Our letters are opened before they're given to us. Mother Immaculata doesn't read everyone's mail but she reads your letters. Mother says you're a real missionary."

"That's what I've come to talk to you about, Kathleen. I want to be more than a volunteer lay missionary. I want to become a missionary sister."

"OH," I said in total surprise.

"I've been thinking of entering an international group of sisters. I came to talk this over with Mother Immaculata and you before making a final decision."

This unexpected visit and news rendered me mind-boggled and unreactive.

My mother went on, "Mother Immaculata asked if I'd consider entering the same congregation as you. I told her that I'd talk to you first. How would you feel if I were to enter the missionary congregation you've chosen for yourself, Kathleen?"

Was I having an-out-of-body experience? My ears heard my mother's question, and they heard my response, "That'll be okay if it's what Mother thinks you should do," but my mind floated out of the room. *Does this mean my mother will become my sister? Bizarre!* By the time my mind returned the allotted time for the visit was up.

"Are you happy here, Kathleen?" my mother asked. "You've lost weight. Haven't you?"

"I'm very happy. I lost weight because I'm pitching hay in the barn."

"What?"

"The summer craft fair will be held in the barn this year. Canonical novices can't attend but we can help with the preparations. We pitch the hay from the entrance level over the beam into the lower level."

"I hope that you wear a mask, Kathleen, when pitching old dusty hay!"

"Oh yes, I've a handkerchief over my mouth and nose as well as one across my forehead. Mother has told us to replace the linen band with a large man's handkerchief whenever we play baseball or pitch hay. She'd rather we use our novitiate training for studying, meditating or playing a musical instrument than starching linen bands. You'll remember, Mum, on my dowry list there was a dozen of men's handkerchiefs. Now we know why."

"Yes, I remember buying them with you," she said with a smile.

"Mother only permits us to pitch hay for an hour a day," I explained.

My mother left knowing I was happily adjusted to convent life. However, her visit left me puzzled and thoughtful.

## Chapter Ten

### SECOND YEAR NOVICE

Neither Sister Rebecca nor I noticed what Sister Samantha noticed. "Don't you listen to what Mother says in the conferences?" she whispered one evening.

"Yeah," said Sister Rebecca. "She often says, 'Be faithful to the duty of your state in life.' and 'Be faithful to the grace of the moment.' Is this what you're talking about?"

"No! Listen. She's been telling us in a subtle way something is about to happen. One of us is going somewhere."

My heart pounded listening to Samantha's self-assured words. The three of us whispered across the large wooden desks in the damp basement. It felt creepy. *Is Samantha psychic? She can't possibly know about the private conversation I had with Mother General eighteen months ago when Mother General came from England to preside over Sister Carmen's perpetual vow ceremony. Yet she's making this prediction that one of us is leaving the USA when we make our first vows.*

Eighteen months earlier Mother General had asked, "Kathleen, what would you have done if you had not entered the convent?"

"Nursing," I said assuredly.

"Oh, of course, your mother is a nurse. Is she not?"

"Yes, Mother."

"If you are to do nursing you will do it in England. Our missions in India and Africa are part of the British Commonwealth. Your British Nursing license would be accepted in either country."

Then abruptly she straightened her posture in the deep-cushioned armchair which hugged her tightly and said, "You are merely a postulant. I do not think we need to pursue this conversation any further. Do you?"

"No, Mother."

I told no one about this conversation; not even Mother Immaculata.

When I recovered from my dazed state I whispered, "Samantha, why would our novice mistress be hinting about one of us going somewhere when we won't complete our two-year novitiate for another ten months?"

"I don't know. Why have our conferences increased from twice to three times a week in the past month?"

"Maybe Mother has more time since the other novices have finished their two years and left the novitiate," suggested logical Sister Rebecca.

I was too pensive to speculate. The natural lull returned us to our workbooks.

During evening recreation Mother Immaculata said, "I have some exciting news to share with you. The local theatre has invited us to attend the preview matinee for *The Sound of Music* tomorrow."

This announcement brought much oohing and awing as well as clapping from the postulants. One jumped up and down with excitement. We novices smiled knowing we couldn't attend.

Mother Immaculata then said, "This invitation is for sisters exclusively. Sister Breda and I have decided novices will also attend."

We exclaimed: *"WOW!"*

Mother said, "You'll replace your white novice veil with the black veil of the professed sisters for this occasion."

As long as a sister has a black veil on her head everyone presumes the sister is professed, that she has pronounced vows of poverty, chastity and obedience and completed a novitiate training. I shook my head in disbelief. *What a practical and resourceful woman. I bet no other novice in any other congregation will attend.*

The Madison Theater in Albany was packed with hundreds of nuns. Shortly after the movie started, I became emotionally linked with Maria. Later, I identified with the oldest daughter in the von Trapp family. I blushed with her when she and her soldier boy danced to *I am Sixteen going on Seventeen*. For those two hours I was a dreamy teenager again. It took days for me to reorientate myself to being a novice.

The following week Mother Immaculata announced, "I've enrolled you in a six-week Montessori teaching course. Every Thursday evening we'll attend a three-hour class at the seminary. This certification will facilitate your entrance into a teacher's training college later should one of you choose to be a teacher."

Prior to leaving the house on Thursday evenings Mother handed the professed sisters' black veil to each of the four first-year novices as well as to Sisters Rebecca, Samantha and me. "Our minivan will provide space for everyone. Sister Breda, you'll sit up front with me, please. You two postulants, seat yourselves on the motor and you six novices, seat yourselves on the two long seats behind the motor. Sister Kathleen, you may sit on the fold-up canvas chair. It should fit between the end of the first long seat and the sliding door."

"Thank you, Mother," I said gleefully.

Every Thursday evening my heart filled with excitement. I pulled up the skirt of my habit, tucking my Franciscan cord and rosary beads inside, and hoisted myself onto the narrow canvas fold-up chair inside the sliding van door. It was like being on safari. I loved the unconventional incognito nocturnal experience.

※ ※ ※

SISTER REBECCA AND I BEGAN to realize Samantha was right. Mother was preparing us for some definite change. One day she said, "Up until now sisters from the American novitiate have remained in the United States on completion of their novitiate. This isn't to say it'll remain this way. We are a missionary congregation. You must be open to God's will when you make your First Profession of Vows."

Temporary Vows of Poverty, Chastity and Obedience are renewed yearly for five years. Then Perpetual Vows are pronounced for a life commitment.

In our basement consultation quarters Sister Samantha said, "We better enjoy our last ten months together before we're separated."

"My parents won't be happy if I leave the United States," Sister Rebecca said. "My family has lived here for five generations."

I remained quiet.

Our speculation ended when Mother Immaculata informed us, "This morning I received a telegram from Mother General who has decided you'll make your First Profession of Vows in two weeks on August 22nd."

Stunned, even though we had been preparing ourselves, we listened distractedly. Sister Samantha demanded, "How can Mother

*My mother (Leona) as a new postulant enters the convent on my first profession day August 22, 1966. We celebrate this moment together.*

General do this? She can't just cut our novitiate by ten months. Doesn't canon law say the novitiate has to be two years?"

"Canon law specifies that there must be a canonical year within the novitiate. It doesn't specify how long the novitiate is to be." Mother Immaculata sighed. With pain-filled eyes she continued, "This is what it means to make a vow of obedience. We must believe God speaks to us through our superiors." She made the sign of the cross on our foreheads. "You may walk around the grounds

*Sisters Rebecca, Samantha and Kathleen have photo taken after the ceremony on August 22, 1966. A week later Sisters Rebecca and Kathleen leave the USA for England.*

until Vespers. I'll announce this to the rest of the community at the end of recreation tonight."

We walked, we cried, we hugged. It seemed too surreal to comprehend.

At the end of recreation while we drank hot chocolate our Novice Mistress tapped her mug with a spoon. "I have important news to share. Sisters Kathleen, Rebecca and Samantha will make their First Profession of Vows on August 22nd of this month.

Furthermore, Sister Kathleen's mother, Leona, will become a postulant on the same day."

Mother raised herself from the low wicker chair before anyone had a chance to react to her announcement. "We'll keep our sisters and Leona in our prayers. As soon as you finish your hot chocolate you may proceed to chapel for Compline."

※ ※ ※

THE FRESH SMELL OF FALLING autumn leaves prevailed on August 22,1966. Mother Isabel, as regional superior in the United States, came to preside over the ceremony. In the chapel after Leona was received as a postulant, Sisters Rebecca, Samantha and I pronounced temporary vows for one year. At which time the three of us received our 'obedience'. When a sister receives an obedience, it means she is 'missioned' somewhere.

Mother Isabel said, "Sister Rebecca, you'll go to Manchester, England. Sister Kathleen, you'll go to Liverpool, England. Sister Samantha, you'll remain here in Upstate New York."

Sisters Carmen, Barbara and Breda gasped. I remembered what Mother had said in her conference. "Up until now sisters from the American novitiate have remained in the United States but it may not remain this way." *I guess Sisters Carmen, Barbara and Breda weren't expecting us to leave the United States.* In their state of shock, they didn't congratulate Sister Rebecca or me.

Nonetheless, Mum and I hugged and congratulated each other. It was a very happy moment for us together and individually.

I whispered to Mum, "I think that I'm going to Liverpool, England to start nursing training. As you know nursing programs start in September. Probably this is why Mother General brought my profession forward."

"Oh, Kathleen, I hope so. I will anxiously await your letters from England."

Chapter Eleven

## LIVERPOOL, ENGLAND

Our B.O.A.C. plane descended onto Ringway Airport runway in Manchester at 0700 hours on August 31,1966. Sister Rebecca, Mother Isabel and I proceeded to customs.

Mother Isabel said, "The sisters from your communities will meet you at arrivals. Sister Kathleen, your sisters will drive you to Liverpool."

"Thank you, Mother."

In the arrival terminal there was a sea of black veils and swinging white cords to welcome Rebecca and me to England. In the excitement Rebecca and I didn't get a chance to say our goodbyes. My novitiate companion with whom I'd exchanged so many ideas during our Saturday morning laundry talks was gone. *When will I see her again?*

"Welcome, Sister Kathleen. I am Mother Elizabeth."

"And I am Sister Martha, the cook."

"Pleased to meet you." *They speak so formally*.

"Our chauffeur is waiting for us outside," said Sister Martha. "Let me take the push cart for you."

*Hmm… Sister Barbara called herself the chauffeur in Upstate*

*New York when she and Sister Carmen met Mum and me at the train station. I wonder if their chauffeur is a Sister Barbara?*

A wide black vehicle was parked alongside the arrival terminal. A male dressed in a professional chauffeur's uniform stood at the front right shoulder of this stately vehicle. He took broad steps toward us. "Let me take that for you, Sister Martha."

"Martin, this is our new sister. Sister Kathleen, this is Martin, our chauffeur and friend," said Mother Elizabeth.

"Pleased to meet you, Martin," I said. Martin tipped his hard-brimmed cap in a professional manner. He bent forward and opened the front car door. Mother Elizabeth lifted her habit with the same poise as would a first lady raise her ballroom gown. She stepped into the front of the Daimler Major and lowered herself into the black leather seat. Sister Martha clumsily got into the left rear seat.

"Sister Kathleen, you may sit on this side," said Martin in a polished English accent.

"Thank you, Martin."

*Why is there a glass partition separating Sister Martha and me from Mother Elizabeth and Martin? Why is the Union Jack flying on the left front shoulder and the yellow and white Papal flag on the right front shoulder?"*

Before I could ask why I was in a diplomatic vehicle Martin edged the Daimler away from the curb into traffic. Tiredness overtook me. I slept until Sister Martha shook my shoulder. "Sister Kathleen, wake up. We are in Liverpool."

Martin opened the rear door for me and stood erect until I passed him.

"You may come this way, Sister Kathleen," Mother Elizabeth said, holding the front house door open for me. "Welcome to the archbishop's house. We are using the main entrance today since His Grace is not home. Normally we use the servants' entrance.

His Grace will return from holidays next week. His auxiliary bishop is handling things in his absence. You will meet him and the rest of the staff tomorrow."

*What is she talking about? What am I doing in an Archbishop's house? Have I been kidnapped? I'm a poor Franciscan sister. Why are our sisters living in a house with plush red carpets, crystal chandeliers, and using a Daimler with a professional chauffeur? Two weeks ago, I pronounced a vow of poverty. Is this poverty?*

Sister Martha set my bags down on the step. "Shall we bring Sister Kathleen to the convent side? I have made a light lunch."

"Yes, of course, let us have lunch," said Mother Elizabeth.

We sat in soft low armchairs in a semi-circle around the fireplace eating daintily trimmed sandwiches, puff pastry cakes, and drinking strong black tea.

"We are happy to have you in our community," said Mother.

Utterly bewildered I managed to say, "Thank you." To my 20-year-old eyes, Mother Elizabeth and Sister Martha were old. They were in their fifties.

*They fuss over me like grandparents over a baby. Perhaps it's how they see me. A baby in religious life. How can I tell them I don't want to be here when they have welcomed me so graciously?*

"Sister Kathleen, let me show you to your room," said Sister Martha.

"I hope you'll be happy living in community with us," said Mother Elizabeth. "You may go and unpack. Have a good night's sleep."

*Wow, my own room. I'm no longer in a dormitory.*

"Thank you, Mother. You and Sister Martha have been so kind to me."

The following morning Sister Martha scurried about the kitchen, her Franciscan cord swinging and hitting the leg of the table as she hastily put a casserole in the oven. "My Lord has invited

Bishop Hold and his secretary, Father Francis, for lunch," she puffed. "I will bring you to Mother Elizabeth. She wants to introduce you to the bishop. Follow me."

I followed Sister Martha to Mother Elizabeth's catchall cubbyhole under the staircase. Mother was bent over on a footstool polishing the sole of a man's shoe.

*Why is she polishing the underside of a man's shoe? Has she dementia? She seemed normal yesterday.*

"Good morning, Sister Kathleen. Let me take you to meet our bishop and His Grace's secretaries."

*Secretaries? Why has he more than one secretary?*

"Mother, why are you polishing the underside of this shoe?"

Mother got slowly to her feet. "It is important for His Grace's shoes to appear new in the public eye. When he genuflects the soles of his shoes are seen. I polish this area below the heel." She turned the shoe over. "When this area is shiny the shoes appear new."

Placing the shoe on the counter, she said, "Before we go, let me show you His Grace's chamber. It is my responsibility to make his bed and see to the cleanliness of the chamber. Your work will be on the first floor in the dining room, His Grace's study, and attending to the front door. His Grace has appointments most days. He will instruct you with whom he will have elevens or high tea at 1600 hours – that is a cup of tea or coffee – and when he will not require refreshments."

While I was digesting my new job description, I followed Mother down the hallway. She knocked on a closed door.

"Come in."

"Father Mario, this is Sister Kathleen, our new sister. She is from the American novitiate but is Canadian."

Father Mario had smiling Italian eyes. Extending his hand, he said, "Pleased to meet you, Sister Kathleen. Please be assured you may count on me for help in attending to His Grace."

"Thank you, Father."

Closing Father Mario's study door Mother said, "Father Mario is His Grace's secretary for engagements. He accompanies His Grace to different functions and events. He makes sure that His Grace doesn't miss a confirmation or a press conference. The biggest event presently underway is the opening of Liverpool Cathedral. It has been in the planning stages since 1962. Completion is scheduled for this spring. It will be a very busy time for all of us but particularly for you. The papal delegate from the Vatican will stay with us. Fortunately, Mother General brought you to England early to prepare for this very important event. This gives us several months to perfect your dining-room skills."

Before I had time to bounce back from this kick in the stomach, another male voice said, "I thought I could hear friendly voices. This must be the sister we've been waiting to meet."

"Yes, My Lord, this is Sister Kathleen," said Mother Elizabeth.

"Welcome, Sister Kathleen. We are happy to have you on our team."

"Thank you, Your Grace."

This caused loud burly laughter from the bishop, and Mother Elizabeth to explain, "Here in England bishops are addressed as *My Lord* and archbishops as *Your Grace*."

"I think we will get on fine, Sister Kathleen. You may call me Your Grace anytime you like!"

I liked the bishop's humour. It helped me to relax.

"There is another person on staff you need to meet," said Mother as we walked away from the bishop. "Miss Maud, this is Sister Kathleen."

"Welcome, Sister Kathleen. Sorry I am unable to greet you in an upright position but the old legs refuse to support me anymore," she said with a twinkle in her smiling eyes. Miss Maud held out both hands and I leaned forward to let her grasp mine between her warm palms.

"Miss Maud is His Grace's personal secretary," Mother Elizabeth said. "She types as fast as he dictates. And no priest comes to the house to meet with His Grace without her approval."

"You give me too much credit, Mother Elizabeth," said Miss Maud. Then turning her head to me, she said, "I am sure I will see you often, Sister Kathleen. I have my elevens and high tea here in my office."

"Yes, I'll look forward to bringing you coffee, tea, and whatever goodies Sister Martha has for you."

"Attagirl," she responded with a wink.

*Not only are the sisters super nice to me but the staff have smothered me with affection. How can I say I don't want to help them or live in an archbishop's house? How can I explain to my mother I was brought to England to help prepare for the opening of Liverpool Cathedral in the spring and not to start nursing?*

Chapter Twelve

# THE ARCHBISHOP'S HOUSE

As my orientation continued Mother Elizabeth outlined my duties. "Sister Kathleen, you need to make the fire in His Grace's study by 6:30 a.m. to have the study warm for His Grace when he enters at 8:00 a.m. After you have made the fire make sure the fireplace screen is in front before refilling the coal bucket in the coal-shed."

"Yes, Mother."

"Between morning prayers at 7:00 a.m. and mass at 7:30 a.m. return to His Grace's study to stoke the fire and add logs. Once you have served His Grace breakfast in the dining room re-stoke the fire and add more logs. The fire should be fine until you bring His Grace coffee at 11:00. At that time you can get more logs and coal from the coal-shed. The high ceilings and many windows cause the logs to burn quickly."

"Yes, Mother. I'll do everything in the order you've said."

"It sounds more complicated than it is, Sister Kathleen. Once you get into a routine it will get easier."

Sister Martha, wearing a white broad-cloth apron over her black habit, ran into the archbishop's study from the kitchen on the convent side. In former times that area was the servants' quarters. "Mother, there is a call for you on the convent phone." She sounded breathless. *All her racing around makes me nervous.*

"I will meet you in the dining room, Sister Kathleen, after I have taken this phone call."

Mother Elizabeth returned to the dining room with a joyful smile. "My niece in Scotland has given birth to a healthy baby boy. It is her first. I am a great aunty."

"Congratulations, Mother."

"Now let me teach you about waiting on His Grace and his guests." She pulled the archbishop's hand-crafted high-backed wooden chair away from the head of the long table and lifted the overhanging Irish linen tablecloth. "See that bump? That is the foot buzzer under the carpet. His Grace will press this buzzer when he wants you to clear the dishes and bring in the next course. The servant's bell box is on the kitchen wall. Individual lights will tell you from which room the buzzer was pressed. Study the box until you're familiar with the different buzzer rings."

I asked, "Do the bishop, Father Mario and Miss Maud have foot buzzers in their offices as well?"

"Yes, that is correct. Once you know who has pressed the buzzer, use the internal phone to ask how you may help whoever pressed the buzzer. Try to avoid going upstairs unnecessarily. You will need to be careful. Hold your habit up when carrying a tray on the staircase."

"Gee," I said. "I find it hard to go up those stairs in this long habit *without* carrying a tray."

"Do not worry, we will practice everything before you have to do anything on your own."

Mother opened the drawer of the Astoria Grand Louis sideboard behind His Grace's high-backed chair. "In here is the sterling silver cutlery you'll need for the various table settings." She plucked off a purple flannel and took out a spoon. "Each piece has the papal flag engraved at the top. I suggest you use Mondays to polish the cutlery. Mondays are His Grace's, My Lord's and Father Mario's day off. You will only have to serve breakfast but won't need to make a fire in His Grace's study until late afternoon. You will have three less trays to prepare for elevens and no waiting on table at lunch hour. The only elevens will be for Miss Maud. Of course, the milk jugs, sugar bowls, teapots, teaspoons and trays should be polished weekly as well."

"Okay, I'll keep Mondays for polishing silver."

Mother drew my attention to the two wine decanters on either end of the sideboard. "Father Mario will refill these Dublin crystal decanters as required. During the meal he will pour the wine for His Grace and himself. These sterling silver dishes in which the decanters sit should not need to be polished more than once a month."

She replaced the purple flannel over the cutlery before closing the drawer and then opened the cupboards beneath the drawer. "Please be extremely careful when removing these glasses. Waterford crystal is expensive to replace."

"Yes, Mother, I'll be careful. I've never seen such beautiful glasses." I slid my fingertips into the smooth cut-glass design and flicked a finger against the rim to hear its chime. *These magical glasses have a strange attraction for me. They're precious. I'll be their protector.*

"You will gradually learn which goblet or glass is required for which drink." She took a tiny delicate crystal glass in her hands. "This is a sherry glass. His Grace and Father Mario have sherry before lunch and dinner. Carry the sherry glasses on a silver tray to His Grace's study before carrying the decanter. When there are several guests Father Mario will carry the liquor tray. While His Grace and Father Mario are dining, remove the sherry glasses and the decanter from the study. And attend to the fire. When His Grace and Father Mario are finished in the dining room, they will have coffee and a liqueur in the study."

We left the dining room and entered the butler's pantry adjacent to the dining room.

Mother Elizabeth said, "You will spend a lot of your time in this pantry, Sister Kathleen. Think of it as your home base. It is from this room you will wheel the wooden trolley into the dining room to collect used cutlery and plates. Once you have closed the dining room door behind you wheel the trolley to the scullery. Unload the dirty utensils and dishes in the scullery sink and add hot soapy water. Use a clean damp cloth to wipe the trolley of any spills or crumbs. Then wheel the trolley to the kitchen."

"Yes, Mother."

"Sister Martha will put the hot plates on the top shelf and the porcelain tureens on the bottom shelf. Except the soup tureen will be on the top shelf. Wheel the trolley to the pantry and wait until you hear the buzzer before entering the dining room. You will do this before and after each course."

I asked, "How many courses are there?"

"Generally, dinner is a four-course meal. Lunch is lighter. The first course is soup. The placemats and silver soup ladle will be on the table. You will bring in the hot bone-china soup bowls and the porcelain soup tureen. This will be followed by the main course. Served in a porcelain potato tureen, a porcelain vegetable tureen and the gold-rimmed bone-china gravy boat. The third course is cheese and crackers. His Grace is fond of Cambrai cheese. Whereas My Lord prefers Stilton Blue cheese, and Father Mario will eat any cheese on the cheese board. The final course is dessert. Sister Martha's desserts are elegant and delicious."

Although Mother was detailed, she wasn't commanding. "You will use this pantry when polishing silverware and ironing the Irish linen serviettes. We send the long Irish-linen table-cloths out for laundering. You will be responsible for ironing His Grace's laundry as well as the bishop's and Father Mario's laundry. This includes their underwear, socks, golf clothes, shirts and bed linen."

My eyes shot open. "Are you teasing me?"

"No. It is what is done here. It is not done for seminarian laundry but it is done here in the archbishop's house. I hope that I have not shocked you."

"I'm uncomfortable with ironing men's underwear and socks," I said.

"Perhaps I could have Sister Martha iron them."

"NO. It's not fair to ask her to do my job. She has enough to do with the cooking and washing."

"Let us leave this for the moment," said Mother. "I realize this job is totally new for you. I do not mean to overwhelm you. I am merely trying to use this time to train you while His Grace is away."

"Yes, I understand."

"Tomorrow I will train you on attending to His Grace's daily appointments with diocesan priests."

"Thank you, Mother Elizabeth, for teaching me. I'll do my best to serve as cheerfully as you do."

"I know you will, Sister Kathleen. Now, go and relax in the garden until Vespers."

It was hard to shut my mind off when talking with God alone in the garden. *Oh Jesus, my heart is heavy. I feel so disappointed I'm in England doing domestic work and not starting a nursing program. Please give me the grace to persevere until the cathedral is consecrated in the spring. This is my goal. Then give me the courage to tell Mother General I entered the order to go to a foreign mission and live poorly amongst the poor. I know you know this, Jesus. Help me to be faithful to this calling. Amen.*

Chapter Thirteen

## CHRIST THE KING CATHEDRAL

The recommendations of the Second Vatican Council were being implemented too slowly for many sisters in Great Britain. A divide resulted. Young sisters, as well as seasoned sisters who had hung in for ten years in anticipation of change to the antiquated convent rules, argued with sisters who resisted change. Sister Martha was in the group who was tired of waiting. To encourage her I said, "Mother Immaculata started us chanting the Divine Office in English three months before I left the novitiate. In the United States, Mass is celebrated in the vernacular and the priest faces the people."

"His Grace will never celebrate mass in English or face us," Sister Martha said.

"Maybe not tomorrow, but won't the bishop and Father Mario influence him to make these changes?"

"I hope so."

"Mother Immaculata made other changes too: no more asking for penances, no more opening the sisters' mail by the superior, and we were allowed to write more frequently to our families."

Sister Martha wrinkled her nose. "Mother Elizabeth and I have heard about these changes but she continues to open my letters. Would you share what you have told me in our community meeting this week?"

"Yes, of course. I don't think Mother is resistant to change. She may not be in the forefront like you or me but she's okay."

"I suppose. But she is more attached to prestige than we are."

I laughed and said, "You've got that right." I bonded with Sister Martha emotionally yet appreciated Mother Elizabeth's calmness.

※ ※ ※

*December 10, 1966*
*Dear Mum,*

*How I look forward to your letters. It was great to read how many aprons you had sown for the autumn fair. I'm happy Mother Immaculata has you sewing and you're not in the laundry. I found it hard doing laundry in that damp concrete basement.*

*Thanks, Mum, for helping me to accept working in the archbishop's house. I try to keep what you said about Jesus serving his apostles at the last supper in mind when I enter the dining room. Some days I can cope with this la-di-da way of life better than other days. The part of this job I'm comfortable with is ushering an anxious priest into the waiting room and staying with him until His Grace is ready to see him. Often the priest asks: "What kind of a mood is His Grace in today?" I tell him, "His Grace looks tired but he's peaceful." I hope these words help to lower the priest's anxiety before the meeting.*

*Oh, I nearly forgot to tell you. I have direct contact with some homeless men who come to the convent back door begging for food. Sister Martha and I swept a corner of the coal-shed last week. We put in a table with a plastic flowered tablecloth, and some old chairs. It allows our coal-shed guests to sit down while drinking a hot mug of tea and eating a double-decker sandwich. They tell me all kinds of stories. But Mum, mostly I can't understand their Liverpool (Liv-er-pud-li-an) accent. All the same I enjoy listening to them. Each one of them grasps my hands in their large rough worn hands and thanks me before leaving. One elderly bent-over man comes every Monday afternoon and always wants me to say an Our Father with him before he leaves. It's humbling.*

*Mum, I hope you'll have a nice Christmas. It'll be your first Christmas in the convent and my first Christmas in England. I'm praying for snow as it won't be Christmas without snow. Bonnie says there's tons of snow in Montreal. She writes weekly to me. I'm sure she's writing as often to you too, Mum. Bless her. Haven't heard from Anthony. He never got over my entering the convent. I hope he writes to you. Must close now as it's time to bring everyone their high tea tray. I'll watch for your letters.*

*Hugs from your loving daughter, Kathleen*

AFTER THE NEXT COMMUNITY MEETING Mother Elizabeth accepted the recommended changes. Chanting the psalms in Latin was romantic but chanting them in English was meaningful for me. I took the words very seriously until, on my 21st birthday in February 1967, when I had to chant, "Now that I am old and grey forsake me not." (*Psalms* 71:18) These words provoked a fit of the giggles from Sister Martha and me and we left the chapel giggling. His Grace asked Mother Elizabeth, "What is so funny?"

When I brought high tea to His Grace's study, he presented me with a very large wrapped box. "Happy 21st birthday, Sister Kathleen."

"Thank you, Your Grace." I was surprised and carried the box to the kitchen to unwrap. It contained four regular-sized boxes of chocolates.

Sister Martha said, "Crikey! I have cooked for His Grace fifteen years and he has never given me a box of chocolates."

I felt Sister Martha's pain and said, "Well, I'm giving you one of my boxes. Now His Grace has given you a box of chocolates indirectly." We laughed and hugged.

My first experience of springtime in England was memorable. It started in early March with flowers on the pathways through the wooded area of the archbishop's grounds. Sister Martha walked by my side. "These are crocuses. They are still pushing their way through the forest floor. In a few weeks we will see buttercups, bluebells, and finally daffodils."

The woods became my spiritual sanctuary in the days before and after Pentecost Sunday, which fell on May 14, and was the day of the opening of Christ the King Cathedral.

On the eve of Pentecost Sunday Mother Elizabeth said, "Martin has taken Father Mario to Ringway airport to receive the cardinal. Sister Kathleen, please be prepared to welcome His Eminence by bending and kissing his ring."

"Yes, Mother."

When His Eminence arrived, I bent forward making sure not to step on his robe or my habit and kissed his ring. *Oh Jesus, help me to get through these antiquated pompous formalities for the next couple of days. I wish I could hide in the coal-shed with my humble guests. I prefer waiting on them.*

His Eminence extended his soft hand under my right elbow to raise me. He gave me a warm smile, which I returned. *Did he hear my thoughts as I kissed his ring? Even though he's the papal delegate he's a gentleman. I like him. He isn't as formal as His Grace.*

The following morning after the entourage left for the cathedral, Mother Elizabeth and I prepared the dining room table for the dinner that would follow the solemn ceremony. "We need to make mitres with these starched Irish linen serviettes," said Mother Elizabeth.

"Really? How?"

"Let me teach you."

We made four mitres and placed one on each of the four salad plates atop the dinner plates at each setting. The mitre's yellow streamers touched the garland of fresh yellow carnations dispersed among snow drops and green vines twining the length of the table.

Sister Martha in her hurried fashion whisked in to announce, "Martin has returned to bring us to the cathedral."

"Yes, we will be right there," responded Mother.

Within the hour we were in the huge circular cathedral with dignitaries and the general public. Because we were "the archbishop's sisters" we were ushered into the reserved pews. Loud pipe-organ music vibrated the stained-glass windows when the clergy and civil servants processed down the aisle. Many solemn words were uttered to consecrate the altar and to remind the congregation that the altar served as a symbol of Heaven's banquet table.

Mother Elizabeth, Sister Martha and I left the cathedral by a side door when the celebration ended. We had to prepare the various high-tea trays for the clergy's return.

"I suspect everyone will be exhausted and will retire to their suite for a nap before dinner instead of going to His Grace's study," said Mother. "Sister Kathleen, bring a high-tea tray to each suite as soon as they arrive home."

"Yes, certainly," I said.

When I knocked on His Eminence's door I heard, "Enter."

Opening the door, I saw His Eminence's feet elevated on the table. He quickly lowered them for me to place the tray down.

I laughed, which made him laugh. He showed me his blistered heels from wearing new shoes. I left him with the high-tea tray but returned with a hot basin of Epsom salt water and heel plasters. He insisted on attending to his own wounds but repeated, "Thank you, thank you."

This incident relieved my anxiety in anticipation of serving the six-course dinner. It turned out I actually enjoyed waiting on these men that ceremonious evening.

Chapter Fourteen

## LEAVING LIVERPOOL

*May 31, 1967*
*Dear Mum*

*How I wish I could be with you today, on your Clothing Day. You must be thrilled to wear the habit with Franciscan cord and beads. I know you're not permitted to have a photo taken as a novice but I wish I could see what you look like with the white starched band and veil. I hope my homemade congratulations card arrived in time for your special day. I'd like to hear about your retreat and the clothing ceremony. How do you like being called Sister Leona?*

*The months of preparation for the consecration of the cathedral are behind us. Serving the six-course banquet to His Eminence, His Grace, My Lord, and Father Mario went smoothly thanks to Mother Elizabeth's support. The summer months in the Archbishop's House are easier for me. I don't have to make a fire in His Grace's study in the early morning nor tend to it all day. It's nice to be relieved of this burden until early October.*

*But now, His Grace is persnickety about the drapes in his study. When I ask: "Your Grace, would you like the drapes drawn? He inevitably says, "I think we could wait another twenty minutes. Don't you?" Naturally, I politely agree. When I collect his high tea tray twenty minutes later, I again ask if he'd like the drapes drawn. He frequently says: "I think we could wait ten more minutes. Don't you?" Mum, this waste of my time going back and forth to His Grace's study to draw drapes frustrates me. I don't know why he can't draw the drapes himself when he's ready. Maybe he thinks we sisters are glorified maids! Sister Martha says he's got all his brass buttons on and he's got all his chairs at home. She tells me these Irish sayings mean that he's smart. He knows how to get others to do what he doesn't want to do.*

*Will close for this time, Mum. Know I love you and hope your time as a novice is beneficial to you. In August I'll see Sister Rebecca. We'll be in a ten-day retreat at our Mother House. At the end of the retreat, we'll each renew our temporary vows for another year. Am looking forward to catching up with her. We haven't seen one another since coming to England. Bye for now, Mum. Much love, Kathleen.*

WHEN I RETURNED TO LIVERPOOL from our Mother House, Mother Elizabeth called me into her cubbyhole. "Sister Kathleen, starting next month you will attend scripture classes twice a week from 7:00 p.m. to 9:00 p.m. until next May. These classes are for the temporary professed sisters in the Liverpool diocese. They will take place in a Merseyside school."

"Thank you, Mother Elizabeth, for arranging this for me."

"You are welcome. Martin will drive you to and from these classes."

"I sure hope he won't be in his chauffeur uniform and he won't drive me in the Daimler."

"I am afraid we have no choice. We do not own a vehicle and Martin is not insured to drive the personal vehicles of His Grace,

My Lord and Father Mario. His Grace insists Martin be in uniform when driving the Daimler."

I walked away with lowered eyes, my arms tucked inside my wide habit sleeves. In the woods I spoke to Jesus. *I can't go to this course in a Daimler driven by Martin in his official chauffeur uniform. It'll set me apart from the other temporary professed sisters. I'll be a spectacle. I don't want to attend these classes, yet I want to have these evenings away from the archbishop's house. I really need to get out of this prestigious lifestyle. I promised YOU and myself I'd only stay until the cathedral was officially opened. The longer I stay the more committed to this place I become. I'll do this course then ask to be removed from here. Jesus, I felt like a hypocrite when I renewed my vows last week in the Mother House. Please forgive me. I won't renew my vows again unless I can live the vow of poverty according to my conscience.*

The sisters in the course didn't shun me for the manner in which I arrived for evening classes. On the contrary, over winter and spring, many expressed their sentiments. "What a privilege to serve in an archbishop's house." "Aren't you lucky to have banquets and important people to attend." "Does His Grace or My Lord ever get angry with you?" "Are they demanding or kind?" "Do they celebrate mass in your chapel?" "Do they ever ask your opinion on current issues?"

Fortunately, there was no time for answering their questions. I don't think they expected an answer anyways. I did say, "We sisters sure get tasty meals after their banquets!" which caused laughter.

One evening Martin drove me to the Merseyside docks after class finished. I was dazzled by the harbour lights, and loved the lapping of waves against the wooden legs of the dock, and the smell of fish. Martin said he had been a fisherman for many years before he married and had a family. Listening to his nostalgic sailing stories magnified my first experience on the docks at night. I started singing the second verse of *In My Liverpool Home*.

*I was born in Liverpool down by the docks.*
*My religion's a Catholic, occupation hard-knocks.*
*At stealing from lorries, I was quite adept*
*And under an old overcoat each night I slept.*

Martin smiled. "I did not know you could sing, Sister. Where did you learn the words to this song?"

"When I was a little girl my father sang Irish ballads to me. I've an ear for Celtic music. This song was written by Peter McGovern but is sung by The Spinners. Haven't you heard it on the radio?"

"Guess I have not," said Martin. "We should head home before we worry Mother Elizabeth."

In May when scripture classes ended, I kept my promise to Jesus and to myself. I wrote to Mother General and asked to be relieved from my duties in the archbishop's house. Instead of replying to my letter in writing, Mother General came to the archbishop's house.

Behind closed doors, I watched her stuff her generous body into a slender rocking chair. I knelt on the cold linoleum floor in front of her. With an air of impatience and annoyance she said, "And what is the reason you do not want to work in the archbishop's house, may I ask?"

Before I could answer she said, "I chose you to work here. Do you think I could have put ANY sister in this position? It is a privilege to work here. Do you not understand this?"

Trembling, I said, "Mother, I never asked to have a privileged position. I entered to work in the foreign missions. I want to do what Pope Paul V1 in the Second Vatican Council asked of us sisters – to live 'a preferential option for the poor'."

"And what am I to do with you?"

"I could work in the Mother House."

"And what do you think our Mother House is? A juvenile detention centre?"

Perplexed by this description I said, "You'd think so because...."

Before I could finish my sentence, she yelled, "HOW DARE YOU CALL OUR MOTHER HOUSE A DETENTION CENTRE!"

Even though tears rolled down my cheeks and wet the cotton dickey inside my black serge habit I defended myself. "I didn't say that."

"DO NOT SAY ANOTHER WORD," she yelled and waddled out of the room. *Yeah, you'd think our mother house was a detention centre because every young sister who speaks up is brought into the mother house. Then no one ever hears of her again. She is dismissed from the congregation. That's what I had been on the verge of saying.*

※ ※ ※

THREE MONTHS LATER, I WENT to the Mother House. It was time for Sister Rebecca and me to renew our temporary vows for another year. I was looking forward to being with my novitiate friend. I needed to prepare her. "Becky, I'm not renewing my vows at the end of the retreat," is what I planned on telling her.

But before I could share this, something unanticipated happened. The assistant mother general asked, "Sister Kathleen, may I have a word with you, please?" She guided me into a cozy parlour with an unlit fireplace. "Mother General is in Africa. She has authorized me, on her behalf, to give you this obedience. Next month you are to commence a three-year nursing program in Manchester."

My heart was pounding with anticipation. "Thank you."

*Okay, I'll renew my vows. I'm going to be a nurse in the foreign missions! Will I go to Africa? Asia? India? Or South America?*

Mother Elizabeth sewed my white uniforms and shoulder-length white veils. I sewed the buttonholes. Both Mother and Sister Martha said how they'd miss me but were happy for me. His Grace, My Lord, Father Mario and Miss Maud expressed similar sentiments. In September I left the archbishop's house. I had such mixed emotions. I wanted to stay with my first community in England and I wanted to leave to study nursing. The truth was, I knew that I had to have a profession before going to the foreign missions.

Chapter Fifteen

# NURSING SCHOOL

*August 15, 1968*
*My dearest Kathleen,*

*I thank God and rejoice with you that you'll start nursing in September. It gives me joy to know you'll share my profession. Nursing has come a long way since I graduated in 1938. I hope doctors today aren't as condescending with nurses as they were in my time. You can count on my prayers for your studies.*

*The annual summer fair was in the barn again this year. The two dozen aprons I made sold before noon. I'll make more aprons for next year's fair. Oh Kathleen, Mother Immaculata now realizes I can't sing. Mother said at choir practice, "Sister Leona, you're not holding the tune." I told her, "My husband used to say, 'Ona, you couldn't carry a tune if you were carrying it in a bucket!' He'd also say, 'No wonder the babies fall asleep quickly when you sing Tura Lura Lura to them.' He was right. I'm tone deaf."*

*On the whole, I'm keeping well and am happy as a novice. I love chanting the Divine Office and spending an hour kneeing in front of the Blessed Sacrament on Sundays before Benediction.*

*Of course, I bring my children and grandchildren before the Lord during this solemn time.*

*Kathleen, I understand you won't have much time for letter writing. Don't worry. Make sure you eat properly and get plenty of sleep. Once you work on the wards your hours will be long and your feet will hurt. I remember it well. I'll close for this time. God Bless you, Kathleen. I love you dearly, Mum.*

On my days off from the hospital I lived in the British novitiate house in the countryside outside Manchester. The building stood alone on an acreage away from the village homes. The inside was dark, due to low-wattage bulbs dangling from high ceilings, cold, due to tiny fireplaces and no central heating, and dreary, due to dark-brown wainscoting on walls and staircases. Such a contrast to the spaciousness of the archbishop's house, with its chandeliers and plush red carpets.

The novice mistress, Mother Eugene, was a well-endowed no-nonsense woman in her fifties. She welcomed me on my first day. "Let me take you to the temporary professed sisters' study on the third floor."

Her firm footing made a squeaking noise on the old timbers as we wound our way up the narrow back staircase in silence to the top floor. She knocked on the study door. Before anyone had a chance to respond, she opened the door with a forceful push. Three temporary professed sisters raised their heads from their books. "This is our new sister. Sister Kathleen will share this study with you on her days off from the hospital."

The three chimed, "Welcome, Sister."

Mother nodded to me. "I'll leave you to your sisters. They'll tell you the rules for living in the novitiate house." She left and closed the door behind her.

*Oh brother, what an old battle-axe.*

"She's like a sergeant-major," I said. "Is the atmosphere in this house always so tense?"

The three sisters nodded.

"Uh-huh," said one. "I am Sister Joseph. I am a second-year music student."

"I am Sister Thomas Francis, a student social worker," said another.

"And I am Sister Moira, a first-year student nurse at the same hospital as you," said the third sister.

"I'm so happy, Sister Moira, to have another sister with me in the hospital."

Sister Moira laughed. "Then you will be even happier to know there are seven sisters from three different congregations in training with us. The matron of the nurses' residence is Irish Catholic. She keeps us sisters together on the same corridor. We have formed a community and support one another through rough days."

"What are the rules Mother Eugene said you'd tell me?"

"The most important one is never to talk to a postulant or novice," Sister Joseph said.

Sister Moira interjected, "It is like we are ghosts! We pass one another in the hallway, refectory and chapel without acknowledgement. It is like we have no physical presence."

Sister Thomas Francis said, "It is lights out following Compline. We have tried to sneak back in here to study but it is freezing without lighting the fireplace."

"I have learned to have my two days off every second week." Sister Moira said.

"What do you mean?" I asked.

"It is expensive to take two buses and a train to get here from the hospital for one day off. Every second week my days off are not together. For that week I remain in residence where I have high wattage light bulbs, a TV room, a ping-pong table and central heating," she explained. "I come to the novitiate house on alternate weeks when my two days off are together."

Like Sister Moira, I too found the journey long between the nurses' residence and the novitiate. After long hours and days nursing, it exhausted me to walk uphill on cobblestone streets in a long habit and cloak with an armful of heavy medical books. In order to wrap my arms around the books I had to first tug the wide habit sleeves through slits in the cloak. When it rained, I cursed the slippery cobblestone and the inside-out umbrella. Even the remembrance of Mary Poppins couldn't make me smile as I trudged along.

Soon I did the same as Sister Moira. I arranged to have my two days off every second week.

In the winter months Mother Eugene advised Sister Moira and me not to commute in the dark. We were happy to oblige! *Fewer nights in the novitiate house to sleep on a thin cloth mattress with a hollow centre.*

Once when I complained about a pain in my lower back due to the mattress Mother Eugene's assistant said, "Uncomfortable bedding is a form of mortification. We should not have the same comforts as worldly people. And while we are on the topic of mortification, you shock our postulants and novices when you take the salt and pepper shakers from the cabinet and place them on the refectory table. And when you genuflect in chapel showing the fur around the heels of your slippers. No one in this house takes salt and pepper. No one has slippers. They have hand-me-down shoes. We train our postulants and novices in the British novitiate to practice mortification. Obviously, the American novitiate does not teach this."

Glowering at her with a pit-bull stare I said, "On the contrary, Mother Immaculata teaches that mortification is an internal sacrifice made between oneself and God. No one should know if I'm denying myself the pleasure of salt or pepper when the shakers are on the table in front of me. One can't practise self-denial if the use of something isn't available. It seems to me your postulants and novices learn endurance but not self-denial. I'm grateful to Mother Immaculata for the deep spiritual formation she gave me."

After that uncomfortable exchange I returned to the hospital.

Chapter Sixteen

## THE UNEXPECTED

Vatican II ended in 1966. The recommended changes came into effect for my congregation in 1969. Some initial changes were: Mother Stephanie replaced Mother Eugene as novice mistress; the novice mistress's assistant position was eliminated; the American novitiate and the British novitiate amalgamated; and a modified habit replaced the traditional habit.

Sister Leona was one of two senior novices to come from the American novitiate to the British novitiate. I phoned Mother Stephanie. "Are you aware that Sister Leona is my mother? And are you aware I spend my days off from the hospital in the novitiate house?"

"Yes, to both questions," Mother Stephanie said.

"I can't be in the same house as my mother and not be allowed to have any contact with her."

"Please do not make assumptions," Mother said. "I have only recently become the novice mistress. Gradually I will introduce changes. Please be patient."

"Okay. Thank you. I'll be home on Friday"

"Then I will look forward to meeting you on Friday, Sister Kathleen."

In the hospital cafeteria, I shared the conversation I had had with Mother Stephanie.

Sister Moira said, "It sure is going to be interesting to see what changes Mother Stephanie is going to make."

"I hope she'll buy us new mattresses!"

"And put high-wattage light bulbs in the place!" added Sister Moira.

For the first time we looked forward to our days off at the novitiate house.

It was raining when I stepped off the train. *Soon I'll see Mum (even if I can't speak with her). What will she look like in the habit, band and veil? Maybe we could wink at one another in the refectory, hallway and chapel. What a strange experience this is going to be for both of us.*

My thumb pressed the latch on the front door in sync with turning my key in the lock. But the door wasn't locked. *Really? Is this indicative of Mother Stephanie's changes?* I opened the foyer door and hung my damp cloak on a hook below the shelf for gloves and scarves. I opened the inside door. There she was: my mother. She hugged me and kissed me on the cheek.

"Welcome home, Kathleen," she said, with a huge smile that deepened her dimples.

"Mum, we aren't allowed to be seen together. What are you doing waiting for me at the front door?"

"Mother Stephanie gave me the job of keeping the entrance clean. I'm legitimately here mopping the floor," she said, winking.

"Oh, Mum, it's wonderful to have you here. All the same we better be careful. I don't know Mother Stephanie."

"She's great," said my mother.

"Well, I'm going into chapel for a visit before I go upstairs to the temporary professed students' study." I gave my mother a little hand wave as I closed the chapel door behind me.

When I exited the chapel Mother Stephanie was descending the wide carpeted front staircase. "You must be Sister Kathleen. Welcome home."

I looked at her in amazement. "Thank you. I've never seen anyone use this staircase."

"It is about time it serves a purpose. It is a staircase besides being a showcase." *She coined that right. It only goes to the first floor.*

"Would you like to join me for a cup of tea? Or if you prefer, coffee? I have created a professed sisters' community room on the first floor. You will remember it was a spare guest room that I believe was never used. I put a sofa and a few comfy armchairs in there."

Trying not to look too stunned by her hospitality I said, "Okay, let me put this armful of books in the third-floor study then I'll come down the back stairs and join you."

In the study I asked Sisters Thomas Francis and Sister Joseph, "What do you think of Mother Stephanie's approach?"

Sister Joseph spoke first. "It is refreshing not to hear the loud brass hand bell every hour. Mother Stephanie asked me what changes she could make to help me. I told her, 'Get rid of the clanging cowbell every hour, please.'"

Sister Thomas Francis grinned. "And I asked her for high-wattage light bulbs."

"Have you seen the professed sisters' community room, Sister Kathleen?" asked Sister Joseph.

"No, but I'm going down there now. Mother has invited me to have tea with her. Catch you up later."

I knocked on the frosted glass in the centre of the antique barn door and heard, "Come in."

Once I was inside Mother Stephanie said, "It is not necessary to knock. This is our community room. I want us professed sisters to have a place to chat, play cards, do jigsaw puzzles and relax together when time allows."

I made myself comfortable in one of the armchairs near the fireplace and hugged the throw pillow.

Mother Stephanie shared, "Your mother has settled nicely into her new surroundings. The young postulants and novices tease her. She will not let them put a dish in the sink until they have wiped the plate free of grease. I hear the giggles as they purposefully put a greasy plate on the counter waiting for Sister Leona to scold them. It is like these youngsters have a mother in your mother being here. It is good for them and it is good for Sister Leona."

I laughed. Mother's account reminded me of my own up-bringing. "My siblings and I always knew my mother wasn't really upset with us if we could see her dimples. If there were no dimples, we knew we'd crossed a line."

Mother topped up my teacup. "How come the hospital gives you and Sister Moira two days off together only every other week? And not weekly?"

I was taken aback by her direct question. "The hospital doesn't. We ask for a space between our days off on alternate weeks."

"Why?"

"Because I find it depressing coming such a long way to a dark, cold place with a tense atmosphere. Sister Moira and I can only handle coming here every other week. Also, the nurse's residence is warm, up-beat, and bright. My room has a lovely rose-patterned bedspread with matching curtains. And it has a firm mattress. Here I can't sleep on the hollow cloth mattress with Sister Polycarp snoring like rolling thunder. I know she's a saintly old nun but I'm sure her snores aren't part of her sanctity."

Mother snickered. "Yes, I have heard her snores and they are excessively loud. She is in that room on her own except when you and Sister Moira are in from the hospital. Finish your tea and we will find you another room."

*Thank you, Jesus, for a common-sense woman and not a religious fanatic.*

Mother Stephanie added, "If you find this place depressing think how depressing it has been for me coming here from sunny South Africa. I would appreciate it if you would come home weekly. I want us professed sisters to have community apart from the sisters in formation. At least let us work together to make each of our situations healthier, holier and happier."

"Thank you, Mother. I'll come home as often as I can."

The following week I came straight home from my fourth consecutive night shift. I had three days off as the first day was my 'sleeping day'. The rocking motion and the click-clackety rhythm of the train put me to sleep. Luckily the novitiate was the last stop on the line.

The conductor gently shook my shoulder. "Sister? Sister?"

Although I was dazed, I managed to say, "Thank you."

The morning air revived me as I shuffled along the cobblestones to the novitiate house. My mother greeted me at the front door again. It was like her heart knew when I'd arrive.

After a chapel visit and a cup of tea with Mother Stephanie and the student sisters, I went to bed. No sooner was I in bed with the curtains drawn than my mother's white veiled head poked through the gap in the curtains. "Kathleen, here's a hot water bottle."

I couldn't help but smile. "Mum, you're going to get both of us in trouble. Novices aren't allowed anywhere near the professed sisters' dormitory."

Ignoring my warning she pulled up her habit, rosary beads and Franciscan cord, and climbed onto the foot of my bed. "Kathleen, what ward are you working on? How do you like it? What interesting cases are you nursing?"

Even though I was beyond exhaustion, I was anxious to share my hospital experience with my mother and I did. We took turns holding the hot water bottle. Then she snuck away and I went to sleep.

Chapter Seventeen

## SISTER LEONA

A week later I watched my mother seated at the novices' table from my professed sisters' refectory table. Her tense jaw muscles indicated to me she was upset. She didn't look over at me as she normally did. She ate quickly and left. After lunch postulants and novices congregated in the conference room for their recreational hour. I opened the conference room door a crack but didn't see my mother. I found her in her dormitory sitting erect on the edge of her cell bed tugging at an embroidery thread. I didn't care if I got in trouble for entering a novice's dormitory. I sat beside her. "Mum, what's the matter?"

"Nothing," she snapped.

"Did Mother Stephanie scold you?"

"No."

"Did you have a run in with a postulant or novice?"

"No."

I faced her and took her hand in mine. "Mum, what's the matter?"

She looked at me. "I'm dribbling. I dribble in the hallways, on the stairs, in chapel, in the refectory, whenever I cough or sneeze.

I have to hand-wash my panties and hope they'll dry overnight in my cell."

I rubbed my thumb rhythmically over her closed hands. "Mum, as a nurse you know dribbling happens when the uterus presses on the bladder. Your uterine muscles have weakened with multiple pregnancies. You need surgery."

"I carry a cloth in my habit pocket to wipe up the drops," Mum said with embarrassment. "I'm like a pup."

"Mum, would you like me to talk with Mother Stephanie and let her know what's happening?"

"Yes. Thank you, Kathleen." We hugged and I left the room.

※ ※ ※

Two weeks later Mother Stephanie phoned me in the nurses' residence. "Your mother is in stable condition in recovery following a hysterectomy."

I breathed out a sigh of relief. "Thank you, Mother, for letting me know. I prayed for her while I worked today. Tomorrow on my split shift I'll visit her. Maybe we'll meet at the hospital. Sorry I have to go. Other nurses want to use this lobby payphone. Bye for tonight."

"Bye."

On the staircase, Jeniece, a second-year student nurse from Trinidad asked, "Have you had any word about your mother's surgery?"

"Yes, she's in recovery and will soon be transferred to a private room on the floor."

"Oh, that's good news. Do you want to go see her tonight?"

"I never thought of going tonight but I sure would love to see my mother."

"Then let's go!" Jeniece said enthusiastically.

At the private nuns' hospital, the attending sister at the front desk asked, "May I help you?"

"I know the visiting hour is over but I wondered if I'd be permitted to see my mother, Sister Leona."

With a quizzical look she said, "We heard that Sister Leona had a daughter in the same convent. Let me phone and find out if she is on the floor." A few minutes later she looked at me with an expression of adoration. "Yes, Sister Kathleen, you may see your mother, Sister Leona."

I was uneasy with the celebrity treatment. *Does she imagine me as St. Therese of Lisieux, the Little Flower, and my mother as her older sister, Pauline? I hope she doesn't take photos. Or broadcast this situation outside the hospital.*

My mother looked frail in the post-op bed. She was a thin woman of short stature weighing no more than a hundred and five pounds when she was well. Tonight, her face looked thinner in the dimly lit room with the top sheet tucked around her chin. As I neared her bedside she opened her eyes. "Oh, Kathleen, how good of you to have come. I'm happy to see you."

"How are you feeling, Mum?"

"Groggy." She gave me a lopsided smile before returning to dreamland.

I kissed her forehead. My lips remained long enough for her to feel comforted and loved.

"I'll phone Bonnie and let her know," I whispered, "that you've come through surgery well."

※ ※ ※

THREE MONTHS AFTER SISTER LEONA'S hysterectomy, Mother Stephanie and Mother General accepted her request to make First Profession of Vows along with four novices from her novitiate

*A treasured memory of standing beside my mother (Sister Leona) on her first profession day (1969). Mum couldn't stop smiling. She was radiant. After Vatican II in 1965, all active congregations were asked to modify/ modernize their habits – hence both my mother and I are wearing the new religious dress.*

cohort. During the ceremony Sister Leona's white novice veil was replaced with a short black veil. The traditional floor-length habit with Franciscan cord was replaced with a modified habit. I saw Mum's dark hair with silver streaks for the first time since she'd entered the order. In my eyes she looked young when she flashed a quick wink in my direction as she knelt before Mother General to receive her obedience.

"Sister Leona, you will live in our Mother House," Mother General said.

Even though my mother's back was to me I heard her say, "Thank you, Mother."

The parents of the four newly professed sisters, Mother Stephanie and I clapped jubilantly before we exited the chapel. In the front parlour we received the five sisters with hugs and congratulations.

Mother Stephanie asked my mother, "Sister Leona, may I take a photo of you and Sister Kathleen together?"

To my surprise Sister Leona said, "That'd be nice."

*What? Mum agrees to a photo? I remember how embarrassed she was on her entrance day and my first profession day when a photo was taken. But today she's too happy to care about any attention bestowed on us as a mother and daughter combo. Her radiant smile reflects her inner peace.*

Within the week Sister Leona left the novitiate house for Broughton Hall Mother House. Broughton Hall was donated to the congregation in 1952 by Mrs. Hall. Its heritage dates back to the 13th century when it was owned by the Broughton family.

*Broughton Hall Staffordshire*
*December 1970*
*Dear Kathleen,*
  *It's such a nice day I thought I'd spend it with you. The*

*Broughton Hall in Staffordshire, England. This 16th century Elizabethan manor was our Mother House from 1952 to 1993. To the left of the entrance door was the kitchen. Above the kitchen was the infirmary corridor. And the stairway to the spooky long gallery on the third floor was to the right of the main entrance.*

*brightness from the winter wonderland outside lights up the interior that is otherwise dark due to the oak wood floors, doors, tables and window seats. I admire the craftmanship in this manor. Do you know the ceiling and wall beams are joined with wooden pegs? There isn't a nail in this magnificent building. I particularly love the wide oak staircase with the mahogany fruit bowl on the banister post supporting the high mounted light jutting upwards from the centre of the fruit bowl. I gaze at it on my way into chapel. I'm told the chapel with its stained-glass windows was one of the smaller ballrooms in the Elizabethan era. Kathleen, I've read many Elizabethan historical novels but never dreamed of living in an Elizabethan manor.*

*The long gallery, of course, was the main ballroom. It's not hard to imagine the Viennese waltzers gliding over the oak floor in this oblong room with their gowns and coat tails. I must admit the long gallery has a spooky aura. Some of the sisters believe a ghost lives in one of the small rooms off the long gallery. Our Irish sisters are great at telling us their banshee stories!*

*Enough about Broughton Hall. What I want to share with you, Kathleen, is that Mother General gave me an obedience to nurse in Kenya, East Africa, in the new year. I accepted this obedience even though I think it's too soon after my hysterectomy to travel. I trust God will keep me safe and healthy. This time next year you'll graduate as an R.N. I'm disappointed I won't be here to attend your graduation. Maybe after graduation you'll nurse in Kenya as well. Wouldn't that be great, Kathleen, if we were together in Africa? I'd be happy to have one of my four children with me. I miss Bonnie, Anthony, Bob and my five grandchildren. They won't be happy when they hear I'm going to Kenya at 56 years of age. I guess none of us expected this obedience. Kathleen, if I don't see you before I leave for Kenya, know I love you dearly. I'll write from Kenya.*

*Tenderly, Mum.*

## Chapter Eighteen

# GRADUATION YEAR

*September 22,1971*
*Kaplong, Kenya,*
*Dear Kathleen,*

*Sorry for the delay in writing to you. I had a bout of Malaria for which I received an intravenous infusion and Quinine tablets. Don't worry I've recovered. The sisters think the infected mosquito attacked me on our road trip to Uganda. I forgot to use repellent.*

*I love the orphanage with the babies and little children. They're beautiful with their shiny brown skin, big brown eyes, and cherub faces. I went with Hanuni on a short outing. It was uplifting. She had the children singing as they walked two by two in front of her. She told me her name in Swahili means 'cheerful'. She definitely is cheerful, always with a big smile emphasizing her high cheekbones. I admire the straight posture of the Kenyan men and women. The women are graceful in their colourful wrap-around dresses and elegant head-dresses which make them appear taller than they are. Maybe I should wear their head-dress instead of my veil! Hanuni taught me a few words in Swahili. I can say 'hello', 'thank you' and 'how are you?'*

*Kathleen, I'm thrilled you're going to Perú with Sister Mariana and her two teacher friends. What an honour to start the first experimental community for the congregation. But of course, it's sad for Sister Ursula who's been diagnosed with tuberculosis. It was kind of Sister Ursula to recommend you as her replacement. You entered religious life to be a missionary. Now your time has come, Kathleen.*

*Have to return to the orphanage. This'll be my last letter. I'll see you in Montreal in eight weeks for your perpetual vow ceremony. I've sent Bonnie my flight itinerary.*

*Kawaheri (Goodbye)*
*Lovingly, Mum*

I WANTED TO GRADUATE, PRONOUNCE perpetual vows and go to Perú, but the decline in women entering the convent and the hundreds of sisters leaving the convent unsettled me. *We're losing our very best sisters. They're in their thirties and I look up to them.*

I asked Mother Stephanie, "Why are sisters leaving?"

"Vatican II emphasized all Christians have a vocation to holiness and intimacy with God whether married, single or a sister. Some sisters feel that their vocation is no longer special and choose to leave. Some older sisters feel betrayed by Vatican II. They do not want the traditional habit to be modified, or the Divine Office to be prayed in the language of the country and not in Latin." Mother paused. "Sister Kathleen, stay anchored in your spouse. Do not compare your vocation to follow God with anyone else's vocation to follow God."

"Thank you, Mother Stephanie. There's another matter that's troubling me."

"Do you want to discuss it?"

"It's a moral dilemma I'm facing on the gynaecology ward. Since the *Abortion Act of 1967* was approved in England, women are coming from neighbouring countries for abortions. Even if I don't personally agree with abortions, I don't feel it's my place to judge anyone who seeks to end their pregnancy."

"Are you being asked to participate in the abortion surgery?"

"No. The problem is that the Catholic nurses won't give a woman her supper the night before surgery or a gown, arm bracelet, or accompany her to the operating room. They watch me do all these things for the woman and are now shunning me."

"Sister Kathleen, why are you doing the things the Catholic nurses won't do?"

"Because I want to treat the woman the same as I treat all of my patients. I feel the Catholic nurses are *so* Catholic they may forget to be Christians.

"I understand. In South Africa I witnessed Muslims put Christians to shame with the love they showed one another," Mother said.

"I think that everyone, even sisters, are guilty of abortion when we choose to ignore another or abort someone out of our life because the person doesn't meet our needs or expectations."

"You are a passionate woman," Mother Stephanie said before adding, "and God needs passionate women!"

※ ※ ※

DUE TO FEWER WOMEN ENTERING the convent, the novitiate house in the countryside outside of Manchester was sold. Mother Stephanie, Sister Joseph and Sister Thomas Francis moved into a cottage convent near the hospital.

I asked Sister Moira for her thoughts, "I look forward to going to the cottage convent on my days off – how about you?"

"I am pleased it is close by. And it is more charming than the acreage house."

The cottage, with its slanted roof and roses climbing between the wooden window frames, invited anyone who gazed upon it to come inside. Our study room was on the second floor while our student bedrooms were in the attic. We no longer had dormitories. My noggin often hit the slanted ceiling if I forgot to bend my neck when bouncing in or out of the high brass bed. A favourite memory is of the full moon casting its beams of light across my bed through the skylight window. In springtime I'd open the skylight and listen to the birds chirping their morning song of praise at 3:00 a.m.

On the day of my final nursing exams, Mother Stephanie said, "The sisters have organized a going-away party for you this evening. Please come for supper at 5:00 p.m. Blessings on your exam. Be confident. God is with you."

"Thank you. I'll do my best. Will look forward to the party this evening. See you then."

After a beautiful meal and a few games of bridge, the sisters gifted me with a blue nylon anorak.

When the party ended, Sister Ursula motioned me to one side. "Kathleen, if Sister Mariana's Peruvian experimental community does not last, you have a place here with us. I deprived you of doing midwifery when I asked you to be my replacement."

She was right in a way: in England midwifery often followed general nursing studies.

"Ursie, don't fret. I've never wanted to be a midwife. I didn't like gynecology which leads me to believe I wouldn't like midwifery either. You spared me!" We giggled and hugged. "You take care of yourself and gain another stone. We better get some sleep before it's time to pray Matins."

After Matins we left for Manchester airport. I took the B.O.A.C. to Montreal.

※ ※ ※

VATICAN II PROPOSED THAT ACTIVE religious women, sisters who work in the community, should pronounce Perpetual Vows at Sunday Mass in their parish church. Only contemplative religious women, nuns who never leave their convent, would continue to pronounce Perpetual Vows in their private convent chapel. I hadn't anticipated my wedding day to be in a large modern church full of strangers in the suburb of Montreal. Besides feeling awkward in the crowded church, the absence of my mother kept me distracted throughout the ceremony.

*Where's Mum? What's wrong?*

I stayed at Bonnie's house and my mother at my oldest brother Bob's house. He and his family were lined up in the second-row of pews but my mother wasn't with them.

At the appropriate time the presiding priest invited Mother Isabel and I to stand in front of the altar facing the parishioners. Mother asked, "Sister Kathleen, what do you ask of the congregation?"

"I ask to become a full member of the congregation by pronouncing Perpetual Vows."

"I accept your request. You may pronounce your vows."

"I, Sister Kathleen Ann Kelly, promise to live in poverty, chastity and obedience for the rest of my life."

Mother Isabel handed me the congregational ring with the three vows inscribed on the inside of the band. I put the ring on my wedding finger.

From the height of the top step, I scanned parishioners' heads in search of my mother… in vain. The parishioners clapped as

Mother Isabel and I descended the altar steps and returned to our pew. Sister Carmen and Sister Barbara hugged and congratulated me. Bonnie and her husband stretched out their hands to grasp mine, as did my nine-and twelve-year old nieces.

The lovely lunch Bonnie had prepared for us was more like a funeral lunch than a jubilant celebration. We were preoccupied with why my mother had not attended my perpetual vow ceremony. Everyone masked their pain for me with smiles; I did likewise. Alone in the dark night I cried.

The next morning, I phoned my mother. "Hello, Mum."

After a few seconds of uncomfortable silence, she said, "Hello, Kathleen."

"Mum, I have a dilemma. Bonnie can't accompany me to the Peruvian Embassy in Montreal. I'm unfamiliar with the Metro. It's crucial I obtain my visa this week. Would you come with me, Mum?"

"Yes, I'd be happy to take you to the Embassy, Kathleen."

When I finished filling in the application at the Embassy, Mum and I went for coffee. She reached across the table for my hands. Holding my gaze, she said in a gentle motherly voice, "Kathleen, I *was* with you yesterday. I wouldn't have missed this big moment in your life. I remained at the back of the church and I left when the organ played the closing hymn. I felt it would be hypocritical to sit with the congregation when I've made the decision to leave the convent."

"Mum, what are you saying?"

"I loved Africa and the Kenyan people but not how some sisters treated the African people. I hope you're not too disappointed, Kathleen."

"Mum, you could never disappoint me. Are you sure this is what you want to do?"

"Yes. I thought about it when I was in Kenya. For that reason, I bought a one-way ticket home."

"Mum, to be honest it's been hard for me having you as a sister. A married daughter doesn't want her mother in her marriage. I wanted you, as an outsider, to think sisters were kind to one another and treated everyone with respect. Now you know firsthand this doesn't always happen. I'd prefer to have you as my mother looking at my chosen life from outside than experiencing it from inside with me."

Mum's dimples deepened and I knew that this chapter in our mother-daughter relationship had ended harmoniously.

# PART III

## MANCHESTER TO TUMBES

Chapter Nineteen

## POST CHILEAN YEARS

In December 1972, Sister Mariana granted my request to fly from Santiago, Chile to New York instead of to England. On my arrival at the Upstate convent Mother Isabel was there to greet me. "Welcome, Sister Kathleen," she said. "We're happy to have you in our community in time for Christmas."

I was grateful she resisted saying, "Now you know why I was reluctant to book your flight to Perú ten months ago."

On Christmas Eve morning we woke to two feet of snow. No doubt it caused havoc for drivers but the snow comforted me. Standing by the window in my nightie I looked at the snow-capped vehicles and roof tops. *I wish I could stop dreaming of violence. Every night every dream is of the violence I witnessed in Chile two weeks ago. I now need this magical scenery to assure me I'm safe.*

But my temporary sense of security was smothered when Mother Isabel told me at breakfast, "Early this morning I received a telegram from Mother General. You're to be in Manchester before the end of this year." There are no words to express the crushing blow this message had on my fragile state. In my re-entry culture shock, following my expulsion from Chile, I desperately needed stability and security. This telegram threatened both. I returned to my bedroom without finishing breakfast. Subconsciously North America linked me to South America. England represented defeat. Defeat of what I couldn't articulate.

*Kathleen, you survived the violence in Chile and the false accusation of being C.I.A. Surely you can survive returning to England. Use your Chilean experience as your measuring stick.* There is no logical explanation for the metaphor. But somehow the trauma was measured in metres and every other obstacle in centimetres.

Disheartened, I boarded the flight to Manchester. I cocked my head against the high, hard winged-shoulder of the airplane seat.

The stewardess stopped at my side. "Sister, may I bring you a beverage? Water, soda, hot tea, or coffee?"

"I'll have a rum and coke, please."

With one eyebrow raised, she said, "Yes, certainly."

There it was, my first act of rebellion. I knew there'd be many more. After Chile, I changed.

Inside the airport I moved like a robot to the carrousel. At 26 years of age, I could easily navigate this situation. I pulled the suitcase with my left hand and balanced the hard-shell guitar case over my right shoulder. At the custom's cubicle a tall dark-skinned gentleman in a Sikh's bright-yellow turban said, "Welcome to England."

I didn't want to be welcomed to England but politely said, "Thank you."

I retrieved my stamped passport, tucked it in the deep pocket of my brown handbag, and proceeded to the arrival area where I saw Mother Stephanie through the automatic door. Then I saw Sister Thomas Francis, Sister Joseph and Sister Ursula when the crowd parted. With sad expressions and no words, they hugged me. Tears filled my eyes.

"I know you must be heart-broken, Kathleen," Sister Ursula said. "You will return to South America. I know you will."

"Thanks, Ursie."

I was riled up having to return to England. But when we got to the car and Mother Stephanie said, "Sister Kathleen, let us place your guitar and suitcase in the hatchback. I will drive you to Broughton Hall," I was furious. Mother continued, "The sisters will drive the Volkswagen to the cottage convent."

I felt my eyes burn with anger. "Broughton Hall is my final destination?"

"I am sorry, Sister Kathleen, that Mother General did not tell you she needs a nurse on the infirmary corridor in the Mother House."

We drove the hour from Manchester Airport to Staffordshire in painful silence. When I got out, Mother Stephanie murmured, "I hope things work out for you."

The sister attending the front door of Broughton Hall Mother House said cheerfully, "Welcome, Sister Kathleen. We have been expecting you. I am Sister Isidore. Did you have a pleasant trip?"

Lips tightly pressed together, I nodded affirmatively.

"Let us take the lift. Generally, we do not use this lift. It was put in five years ago to accommodate our sisters in wheelchairs. Oh, would you like to make a little visit to the chapel?" It was customary for a sister to visit the chapel as soon as she arrived in the convent.

"No. I need to go to bed," I said. *I'm too mad at God and Mother General to go to chapel.*

"Of course, Sister Kathleen. You have had a long journey." She pulled open the grill door. "We are both petite. But maybe you could hold your guitar case upright close to your body? Here we go."

I stared through the grill as the lift ascended slowly; it hiccupped when we reached the second floor. I wheeled my suitcase over the oak-wood floor along the dark narrow hallway.

"Here is your room, Sister Kathleen." She opened the door. "You may turn on this floor heater to take the chill out of the air. Please do not move it from this sheet of metal, and unplug it before you get into bed or when you leave the room. I put a stoneware foot warmer in your bed. I hope that you have a good sleep."

"Thank you, Sister Isidore."

"You are welcome. We are grateful to have you take over the infirmary corridor. Sister Andrew leaves for her three-month home visit to Scotland in two days. She will arrive home for Hogmanay."

"Sister Isidore, is Mother General home?"

"No, Mother is not here at present. She returns from India in two weeks. Now, you get some sleep, Sister Kathleen. Good night." Sister Isidore closed the door softly.

*When Mother General returns, we'll have a royal battle if she thinks I'm staying here to do geriatric nursing. She can no longer use the vow of obedience to coerce me into blind conformity.*

In Chile, Sister Mariana had introduced me to Che Guevara and to Karl Marx. I knew young men wore Che T-shirts because they held him up as a hero. He was a hero for Cubans, Mexicans and South Americans. Che knew that medicine alone would not remove the sickness or poverty caused by class distinction and oppression. I had incorporated Che's and Marx's philosophy of equality. *I'm betraying the poor in this upper-class society of convent life with three meals a day, elevens and high tea. Before South America, I hadn't seen naked poverty. But now I have.*

While waiting for Mother General to return from India, I cared for the elderly sisters on the infirmary corridor. It was easy to become attached to these women, who had nursed or taught for twenty and thirty years in mission countries before and during WWII. I loved listening to their courageous stories.

Mother General returned and we met to discuss my future.

"I'll continue to nurse on the infirmary corridor on condition you obtain a place for me in a midwifery program asap."

"And since when did you want to do midwifery?" Mother asked curtly. "You made it very clear when you graduated as an R.N. you had no desire to study midwifery."

"You've got that right. I still don't want to be a midwife. But the two sisters in our only mission in South America say they do not want nurses without midwifery. If midwifery is a requirement for me to go to Perú, so be it."

Mother smirked. "I appreciate your frankness, but I do not make deals with a sister. I need to remind you of your vow of obedience, Sister Kathleen. Continue on the infirmary corridor and I will think about whether you will study midwifery or not."

*Kathleen, let it go. Abide your time. Fight wisely for what you really want.*

"Thank you, Mother."

Chapter Twenty

## MIDWIFERY

I started Part I Midwifery in Manchester. Part I would take six months to complete as long as I was successful in my final written exam. I would have to participate in three assisted deliveries (a registered midwife's hands guided the student's hands delivering the baby's head), three unassisted deliveries, and conduct fifty vaginal examinations (determining the presentation and position of the fetus as well as examining the bony pelvic structures) to qualify me to take the exam. If unsuccessful, I would have to wait three months to take the exam again. This was my double destiny.

When I failed the second time, the senior instructress asked, "Nurse Kelly, is your nunnery making you study midwifery?"

"Midwifery is my passport to Perú."

"I thought as much. You have two left hands. I advise you to give up midwifery."

"I'll master it," I replied. And left Manchester for Lambeth Hospital in London.

The midwifery instructress there was a creative Anglican nun. She directed us six students to form into pairs on the classroom floor. "One of you in the pair is the bony pelvis and the other is the fetus." The pelvis student knelt with her palms on the floor, back arched, forming a canal though which the fetus student crawled. The roles were reversed so each student could experience the birthing process.

As the fetus, I twisted and turned my body to lower my head with each contraction. Sister announced, "Mother is having a contraction."

I couldn't get through the canal until my chin was tucked tightly against my neck.

In this position the baby's head presents with the smallest diameter, which allows baby to enter the birth canal. A larger diameter could possibly lead to a forceps delivery or a Caesarean section.

Sister said, "This maneuver should demonstrate to you that the fetus has to position itself to enter the birth canal. Your job as a midwife is to monitor the fetal heart rate while the fetus positions itself. Keep your hands off the baby's head until the head is fully outside the vagina. Put your hand under the baby's head to prevent the weight of it from damaging the perineum, the muscle tissue between the vagina and rectum."

For the first time I understood the relationship between the baby and midwife. I no longer felt solely responsible for the baby's delivery. Fear of midwifery left me.

Confidently I took the written exam and was successful. I returned to Manchester to commence Part II of the midwifery program – three months in the maternity hospital and three months "on the district."

On the district a midwifery student attends home births with her district midwife. The student midwives got together to praise or criticize their district midwife according to how easy or difficult she was to work with and what kind of a car she drove. The younger district midwives with sports cars were rated the highest.

By unanimous agreement the oldest district midwife, who drove a small beige Volkswagen, was 'The Grinch.' She merited this title because she asked students to attend a birth either after hours or on days off. I hoped to be assigned to a young district midwife with a sports car. *It'll be my only chance to drive in a sports car. Oh, how exciting and fun that'll be.*

When it was my time to start my district training, the district midwifery supervisor (DMS) called me into her office. "Sister Kathleen, I am assigning you to Mrs. Doherty. If you are going to work in remote areas of Perú where you may not have access to hospitals, you will need to develop very accurate midwifery skills. No other midwife has the experience Mrs. Doherty has. You'll start on the district this Monday morning at 9:00 a.m."

"Thank you." *Trust me to win the lottery with The Grinch for my prize.*

The DMS added, "You will not attend maternity cases on Tuesdays. Mrs. Doherty knows that Tuesdays are your study day, but she will try to persuade you to attend a case on Monday night or Tuesday night. You are to refuse. Remember you're a student midwife, Sister Kathleen, not a qualified midwife. Am I making myself clear?"

"Yes, Sister. I won't work on my study day, nor on my time off."

"Fine. You may start on the district with Mrs. Doherty."

On Sunday night the student midwife completing her district training should have given me 'the district phone' but she didn't. This turned out to be one of life's small miracles. Early Monday morning I set out for the clinic on the standard bicycle to meet Mrs. Doherty. I had to walk the last steep slope. The bicycle had neither gears nor hand breaks. Sweat rolled down my temples underneath my veil as I pushed.

Alongside a small beige Volkswagen waited a district midwife in a dark blue uniform with a matching pill-box hat. *That's got to be The Grinch. Heck, she's no bigger than I am. Surely, I can handle her. I thought she'd be six feet tall weighing 200 pounds.*

As soon as Mrs. Doherty spotted me, she sucked in her tight sixty-year-old wrinkled cheeks and spluttered through thin lips, "You must be Kelly. Where were you last night? I tried phoning you but there was no answer. You missed a maternity case. I had to deliver the woman alone. Get into the car. We are going to see the mother and baby."

After a ten-minute drive we arrived at a cottage. Mrs. Doherty pulled the string attached to the copper bell.

"Come in, Mrs. Doherty," the new mother called out.

Our feet were barely on the entrance mat when Mrs. Doherty said, "Now this is the student midwife who should have delivered you. She says that she missed my call because she didn't have the district phone! A sorry excuse."

The mother smiled compassionately at me.

I said, "Sorry I missed the birth of your baby. I'm Nurse Kelly."

"Pleased to meet you, Nurse Kelly. I am Caroline and this is my son, Christopher, named after my husband's father."

Mrs. Doherty said, "Kelly, you may attend to the baby while I attend to Caroline."

From Caroline's house we drove to other mothers who had delivered babies in the last ten days. After these post-natal visits, we returned to the clinic where Mrs. Doherty introduced me to her colleague district midwife, Mrs. MacPherson. "Kelly, this is Mac," she said. "Mac, this is Kelly."

"Welcome to the district, Nurse Kelly," she said. "We have been told that you are going to Perú when you finish your training. How interesting that will be. We will whip you into shape!"

For the first time I saw Mrs. Doherty smile. I sensed that Mrs. Doherty and Mac were good friends.

*What a blessing Mrs. Doherty couldn't reach me last night. If I had gotten the phone call and told Mrs. Doherty I wasn't on the district until 9:00 a.m. today and refused the maternity case, it'd have created a chasm between Mrs. Doherty and Mac and me. I was prejudiced against her from what the students said about her. Thank you, Lord, for protecting me.*

This incident taught me a life-long lesson: to make my own evaluation of a person.

After my first day on the district, I realized that the student midwives had inflated Mrs. Doherty's disadvantages, while obliterating her attributes. She was not young and had no sports car but I would soon learn she was a woman who held both her patients' and her students' interests above her own.

Before cycling back to the residence, I said, "Mrs. Doherty, I want to attend as many births as possible with you. I need as much experience as I can get before going to Perú. Please call me for everything – even on Tuesdays. No study day can replace practical experience."

Mrs. Doherty gave me a brief smile. "A student after my own heart. Yes, I will keep you busy, Kelly."

And so ended my first day 'on the district.'

Chapter Twenty-One

## HOME BIRTHS

On my second district day Mrs. Doherty phoned. "Kelly, one of my prenatal women complains she's having bouts of diarrhea. She's eight months pregnant. So far, she hasn't had any contractions. I'm going to pay her a visit. Do you want to come?"

*Hmm... do I want to go out to visit a woman who's had the runs because of eating too much fruit or drinking curdled milk in her tea?* No, I didn't feel like going nor did I think it necessary. But as a sister I suppressed my feelings. "Yes, of course."

"I'll pick you up in ten minutes. Be at the back door in the parking lot."

After introducing me to the expectant mother, Mrs. Doherty said, "Mrs. Nguyen, would you please lie on top of your bed. I'll check baby's position and heart rate." She listened to the fetal heart with a metal trumpet. "Baby's heart is strong and regular. Now I'll feel your bump for baby's position." A midwife wants to locate the fetal head as it tells her the position of the baby. If the head is low, baby will be born head first. If the head is high, baby is in a breech position.

Then to my complete surprise Mrs. Doherty said, "Kelly, scrub up. I want you to do an internal examination."

I scrubbed my hands and arms in the basin of warm soapy water. Over my surgical mask I watched Mrs. Doherty. With her thumb and index finger she was moving the low fetal head.

I said, "Mrs. Doherty, I assume this is the fetal head you're moving?"

"Yes, it is."

"Then why are you asking for an internal examination if the fetal head isn't in the pelvis and Mrs. Nguyen isn't in labour?"

"We need to know if the diarrhea has caused the cervix to dilate."

*That makes sense but I doubt it. Or is this the voice of experience speaking?*

I gently inserted the index and middle fingers of my right hand into Mrs. Nguyen's vagina. I don't have long fingers, yet my middle finger touched a soft fetal head. Keeping my fingers still, I used my left fingers to move externally the fetal head that I had just seen my midwife moving. The head that wasn't in the pelvis. I looked into Mrs. Nguyen's eyes. "Do you have twins in your family?"

"I don't think so."

"Kelly, what are you saying?" Mrs. Doherty asked.

"I'm saying the fetal head I'm moving with my left fingers is not the fetal head my right middle finger is touching."

"Kelly, withdraw your fingers."

As Mrs. Doherty scrubbed to re-examine Mrs. Nguyen, I whispered, "I think the placenta is near the cervix."

I had never felt pulsation on a vaginal examination before examining Mrs. Nguyen. Pulsation could only be from a low-lying placenta or a cord presentation. Both indicate danger if labour should start. Mrs. Doherty's examination confirmed undiagnosed twins and that the placenta was beside the first baby's head at the edge of the cervix.

Mrs. Doherty acted calmly but quickly. She phoned for an ambulance. While Mrs. Nguyen was pre-occupied with the paramedics, she phoned the hospital suggesting they prepare for an immediate Caesarean section.

En route to the hospital she said emphatically, "Kelly, this is a district case. I'll make sure you're in the operating room. You make sure you receive one of those babies. Don't let any hospital student midwife or registered midwife prevent you. This is your case. Don't let the hospital staff take it from you."

I laughed and said, "I sure won't." And I didn't. I received in my arms one of the twins within seconds of the surgical incision into Mrs. Nguyen's uterus. An unforgettable first maternity case on the district with Mrs. Doherty. Now I understood why the DMS had said, "No other midwife has the experience Mrs. Doherty has."

I learned two valuable lessons that night. Never to dismiss an expectant mother's complaint and to trust my increasingly accurate vaginal examinations. This maternity case more than any other in my training confirmed my diagnostic skills. After this case, it was as if neither Mrs. Doherty nor I saw me as a student in training. Our relationship shifted from student and supervisor to budding midwife and seasoned midwife. We respected each other and our mutual commitment to midwifery.

Mrs. Doherty gave me more responsibility. She'd remain in her car while I assessed the expectant woman in labour. After twenty minutes she'd enter the house and ask for my report. If I reported our patient to be in labour with nothing abnormal to note, Mrs. Doherty would say, "Kelly, give her the 3 aitches." (High, Hot, and a Hell of a lot.) This meant an enema via a can and hose. Mrs. Doherty would then go back to the clinic. She'd only return when I phoned to report the woman would probably deliver her baby within the hour. Being alone with a labouring patient prepared me for the transition from student midwife to nurse-midwife on my own in Perú. Mrs. Doherty's confidence in me helped me to believe in myself.

The DMS phoned, "Nurse Kelly, you will soon be leaving us for Perú. I am permitting a gynecologist to teach you how to suture an episiotomy."

In the delivery room, Dr. Bhatt was full of information about the surgical incision of the perineum during labour. "Sister Kathleen, you need moderate thread tension. Too much tension will cause swelling. Swelling causes pain. A woman in pain will have a difficult time bonding with her baby postnatally. Bear this in mind and you'll suture with the correct amount of tension."

A few years later this skill would save a woman's life at 3,812 metres on Lake Titicaca, in the Peruvian Andes. When you accompany me around the highest navigable lake in the world, you'll learn how this came to be.

In addition to suturing under Dr. Bhatt's supervision, I was permitted to assist him in breech presentations. He taught me how to keep the baby warm as the feet and legs leave the birth canal. "Keep a towel around the vagina area receiving the baby inside the towel. If cool air touches the baby's skin, baby will try to breath. Remember that the baby's head is inside the uterus."

I watched intently and prayed the baby wouldn't breathe until outside the womb.

Dr. Bhatt said, "Remove the towel for delivery of the baby's head." He showed me the technique of slowly delivering the back of baby's head. I assisted Dr. Bhatt in three or four breech births, but only in Perú would I deliver breech births unassisted and in unfavourable conditions.

The district section of Part II Midwifery proved to be the most rewarding and valuable time in my training. The experience of home births was entirely different to the experience of hospital births. In the patient's home I relaxed in the intimate relationships with the patient, her significant other and myself. The subdued but adequate lighting soothed the labouring mother, allowed her to rest between contractions, and had a calming effect on me. In hospital births I was tense. I attributed my tension to: the high traffic of midwives, students and physicians entering and leaving the delivery room, the bright hot overhead lights, and the atmospheric noise. Once the fetal head crowns, the delivery room turns into a football stadium with colleagues in the rafters shouting: "Push, push, keep it coming, that-a-girl, you're a champ, push, push."

On the district I appreciated how the baby, mother and I worked together as a team without a cheering squad. I guess one could say it was on the district with Mrs. Doherty and Mac that I found myself professionally.

## Chapter Twenty-Two

# LOVE ON THE DISTRICT

Getting immunized brought love into my life. I had to be immunized against typhoid and paratyphoid fever prior to returning to Perú. This vaccination caused considerable swelling of my right arm and a high fever. The parish priest whom I knew from attending mass suggested that I stay in the presbytery where his housekeeper could provide me with meals and drinks while I rested. Mrs. Doherty and Mac encouraged me to accept Father Drew's offer since my convent was outside the district boundary. I agreed. In forty-eight hours, the fever subsided but the bump, hard as an avocado seed, limited my arm movement for the next four days. Mrs. Doherty picked me up daily at the presbytery and drove me to the maternity clinic where Mac worked. I did minimal work that final week on the district but at least I had no absenteeism on my record.

In the evenings, Father Drew and I prayed Vespers together before having a game of chess over a glass of Bristol Cream Sherry. My brother Anthony had taught me to play chess when I was eleven-years old and he thirteen. I didn't play it again until I played with Father Drew. Needless to say, he won every time.

When our chess game was over, we prayed Compline. At the end of Compline, Father read aloud John Henry Newman's poem *Lead, Kindly Light*. It was a peaceful way to end the day. Upstairs Father went to his bedroom and I to the guest bedroom which had a lovely view of the countryside from the bay window. Father Drew was six years my senior and had prematurely greying hair. A pleasant looking man of medium build and height.

Mrs. Doherty phoned at 9:00 p.m. on my third recovery evening when Father Drew and I were playing chess. "Kelly, I'll pick you up in ten minutes. Irene has finally started labour."

It was a relief to hear. Irene was pregnant for the second time and five days past her due date. I'd been to her tenement complex several times for her pre-natal care. Oodles of poorly clad children always ran to greet me – the little boys pushed one another out of the way in an effort to carry my maternity box up the concrete stairs, while the little girls reached to hold my hands.

"Is Ma'am Evans having her baby today?" these streetwise little ones asked.

Each time I said, "Not today. Baby's sleeping."

I was happy that Irene had gone into labour when the children themselves were sleeping. I knew they'd have a string of questions when I returned tomorrow. But for tonight, Mrs. Doherty and I focused on delivering Irene's baby. She laboured for five hours before she was ready to push her baby out of the womb. When baby's head was free of the vagina, I felt the umbilical cord around baby's neck. It wasn't loose enough to slip over baby's head. With two clamping forceps an inch apart, I cut the cord between the forceps, and with Irene's next push baby was born at 2:47 a.m. It was a second boy for the Evans family. As a precaution baby was taken by ambulance to the Neonatal Intensive Care Unit for observations. Irene and Robert worried as they softly cried in each other's arms. After attending to Irene, Mrs. Doherty and I went to the hospital to see baby.

The NICU nurse said, "Your baby is doing fine. He was given oxygen then pinked up quickly. Parents may come and bring him home."

We called to give Irene and Robert this wonderful news before we headed home.

I returned to the presbytery at 4:20 a.m. and tiptoed up the carpeted stairs in my stocking feet so as not to wake Father Drew. In the guest bedroom, the bedside lamp was lit and the counterpane turned down. It gave me such a warm feeling of being cared for. Then I saw his note on the pillow. It was simple but loving. *Katie, I hope all went well at the baby's birth. I missed not praying Compline with you. But you were in my heart as I prayed it and read the hymn Lead, Kindly Light. Have a good sleep. Drew.*

I hadn't felt this inner glow before. I really didn't know what I was feeling. *Why is my heart racing and why are my cheeks flushed?* Whatever the warm fuzzy feeling was, it helped me to sleep, knowing I was smiling.

The Wednesday before Christmas 1974 was my last working day on the district and living in residence. Mrs. Doherty and Mac invited me to a pub for lunch. During the meal they handed me a rectangular multi-coloured wrapped gift with a red polka-dot bow on top. The shiny aluminum box, lined with white cotton buttoned to the lid and bottom of the box, contained stainless steel instruments. I was thrilled to have my own professional maternity equipment. Joyful but teary-eyed I hugged them with gratitude. None of us wanted our time together to end.

"Kelly, I have a confession to make," said Mrs. Doherty. "When I heard I was getting a nun for my next student I told the DMS I didn't want a nun on the district with me."

Mac chimed in, "And I didn't want a nun either as I'm a smoker and swearer."

"Sorry, Kelly," Mrs. Doherty said, "but we've had unpleasant experiences that prejudiced us against you. But you aren't the type of nun we imagined. You're very human and not at all sanctimonious."

We laughed.

I said, "And I too have a confession. I didn't want to be with you either. I wanted to be with a young midwife with a sports car."

Again, we rocked in our chairs with laughter. We ended the lunch with Mrs. Doherty promising to see me off at the airport on Friday. "Now let me drive you to the residence for the last time."

Father Drew phoned and asked, "Katie, would you like to come over? I could pick you up? It's your last night so I thought we could celebrate. I've ordered in pizza. I'll drive you back by 10:00 p.m."

"Sure. Pizza sounds good. I'll wait in the parking lot."

"I'll be there in ten."

At the presbytery, he led me by the hand into the parlour where flames danced in the fireplace and the Christmas tree lights twinkled. The warmth of his hand gave me the same fuzzy feeling I'd felt when I read his note. He offered me a glass of sherry. We sat by the fireplace in comfortable silence.

Then he said, "Katie, I wouldn't let you leave on Friday if it wasn't for God. We're both in God's ministry but I love you." He leaned forward and kissed me on the forehead.

I didn't know how to respond or what to say.

"Katie, weren't you aware of my affection for you?"

"No, you're affectionate with everyone."

He smiled. "Katie, I'm not affectionate with others as I am with you."

I took another sip of sherry. "I thought sisters and priests who fall in love are unfaithful in their prayer life. I'm faithful in my prayer life as you are."

"Katie, you're a woman. Being a sister doesn't mean you're not an attractive female."

I blushed. "I guess in my dedication as a sister I never thought of myself as an attractive woman. I've never been the flirty type even before I entered the convent." I felt embarrassed talking about sexuality with him yet he was comfortable with his identity as a man and as a priest.

*How come I'm uncomfortable with my femininity? Did I unconsciously spiritualize my womanhood?*

I said, "Perhaps I've been too focused on becoming a missionary sister and have ignored being a woman too."

He took my hands in his. "Katie, I'd never ask you to forfeit your missionary life. Nor would I stop being a priest. A married priesthood is coming. When it happens, I'll come and be with you wherever you are."

Still overwhelmed and uncomfortable with my own emotions, I joked, "Okay, that'll work."

For the rest of the evening, we cuddled by the fire listening to Mozart and eating pizza.

Friday noon the sisters drove me to the airport where Mrs. Doherty, Mac and Father Drew waited for me. Before going through customs, I hugged each of them. As I hugged Drew, he slipped an envelope into my pocket. His love letter made leaving England a little easier. I re-read his letter many times on the flight to Montreal. My heart knew I already missed him.

But at the same time I was looking forward to spending Christmas with my family and going to Perú in the New Year.

## Chapter Twenty-Three

# A FISHING TOWN IN NORTHERN PERÚ

I pleaded with the pleasant, brown-eyed brunette attendant standing in front of the electronic screen. "Are you certain there isn't a seat on this Wednesday's flight?"

In a beautiful Québécoise accent she said, "Seas... der, dee flight to Lima, Perú dees Wednesday is full. But dhere's a seat on Wednesday February 12th flight. It'll arrive in Lima on dee 13th. Would you like me to book you a seat on dees flight, Seas... der?"

There was nothing I could do to change my fate. I booked the flight and returned to my mother's apartment.

"Mum, I don't want to arrive in Lima on February 13th. It's the same date I arrived in Lima three years ago."

My mother handed me a mug of hot apple cider. I sat at her kitchen table with the mug nestled between my fingers staring at her foot-tall white tulle Christmas tree standing elegantly in the centre. The tree bent itself closer to me and said, *Why are you downcast in this festive season? Look at me with my red ribbon bows on my white stiff branches and be of good cheer!*

Mum said, "Trust and all will be well."

*If only I could be as confident as my mother and her tree.*

The sun shone on Lima airport's runway when I descended the metal stairs. I smiled at fellow passengers, I smiled at the stewardess, I smiled at porters. I couldn't stop smiling. My cheeks were sore but I was too happy to care. The scent of salty sea air told me *estoy en mi tierra, I'm home*. I was tempted to kneel and kiss the ground when I saw Sister Immaculata inside the terminal. Sister Immaculata was no longer Mother Immaculata, no longer my novice mistress. She no longer held a position as superior which meant the designation of Mother was relinquished. I walked through the parted automatic glass doors towards her smiling blue eyes and we embraced.

"Bienvenida, Sister Kathleen, I've been counting the days 'til your arrival. It's great to have you join our community in the north."

"Thank you, I'm ecstatic to be back on Peruvian soil."

"Yes, I bet you are."

"Que alegre soy. He sonado con este momento." (How happy I am. I've dreamed of this moment.)

"I understand, Kathleen. Your heart never left Perú. Only your body went away."

"Tienes razon." (You're right.) It felt wonderful to speak in Spanish.

"Come, let's go to the convent where I board while I'm in Lima."

"How far from Lima is *our* convent?" I asked.

"It's a twenty-hour bus ride north. A beautiful journey. If you're seated on the left side behind the driver, you see kilometres of ocean waves. If you're seated on the right, you may get a glimpse of the Cordillera range of the Peruvian Andes in the distance."

"I've heard about the Cordillera Blanca, the snow side, and

the Cordillera Negra, the green forest side of this range," I said. "Fascinating."

"Yes, indeed. It's a marvellous wonder of nature."

"How many sisters are in the community?" I asked.

"We'll be five when you join us. The superior, Mother Fidelis, and I work with the church youth group. She does crafts and I teach Catechesis. I also chauffer when needed. Sisters Killian and Adriana provide pre-natal care and attend home births."

While I was unpacking at the Lima convent, Sister Immaculata described the community's living conditions. "Besides us sisters, there is a Diocesan priest. He had the house built for us and himself four years ago. We rent from him. It's a long bungalow and he has one side and we have the other. We share a wide veranda facing the ocean. Unfortunately, Father Aled has the habit of making himself at home on our side of the bungalow. I personally find this difficult as his personality is erratic."

"What do you mean by erratic?"

"He seats himself uninvited at our table during meals or in an armchair if we're playing scrabble or having a community meeting. He joins in our conversation while puffing on his pipe. He starts to speak in an amicable voice but ends up shouting and cussing and then storms out of the room."

"Does this happen often?"

"Yes, pretty regularly."

"Doesn't Mother Fidelis tell him he has to respect the sisters' privacy?"

"No, she tells us to remember he's a priest and as such God's representative."

"WHAT? What century is she living in?"

"Mother Fidelis is in her late sixties and from the old school. But she is a beautiful woman and Superior."

"How about the other sisters? Don't they say anything?"

"No, the sisters are European like Father Al. They tell me, 'Europeans are emotional hot-blooded people. Not like you cold Americans.' There is little I can do to change the situation."

"Are these sisters also in their late sixties?"

"No, they're in their early sixties. I'm the youngest at 59," said Sister Immaculata with an apologetic smile.

"Wow, that means everyone is 30 to 35 years older than I am!"

"I'm afraid so, Sister Kathleen."

I placed some clothes in the cupboard before asking, "How come you do Catechesis when you're a midwife?"

"Sister Killian and Sister Adriana prefer to work together. They only allow me to attend a birth if two women are in labour at the same time. In which case, Sister Killian circulates between the cases."

"Hmm," I said. "It sounds like the community situation is difficult with Father Al and the work situation difficult with Sister Killian in control. I hope that I can cope with this mission as well as you, Sister Immaculata."

"I hope so too. At least there's now two of us American-Canadians!" She winked.

Sister Immaculata returned to the north. I remained in Lima to complete the paperwork and obtain my residential permit. A week later I took the all-night and all-day bus ride. I woke in the larger cities of Chimbote, Trujillo and Chiclayo when new passengers boarded. In Trujillo, roughly the half-way point between Lima and Tumbes, I got off the bus to get a breath of air and stretch my legs. *Just twelve hours to go.*

The convent was in the department of Piura. As soon as I stepped off the bus I heard the crashing ocean waves and smelt the salty sea air. A few bare-footed fishermen were mending their nets.

Sister Immaculata introduced me to Mother Fidelis, who

greeted me affectionately and said, in her musical Swiss accent, "You're most welcome to our community, Sister Kathleen."

Sister Killian grunted, "Welcome," with no embrace.

Sister Adriana smiled but said nothing.

*Hmm, I guess this sets the tone for our working relationship.*

Supper was eaten in an uncomfortable silence until Sisters Killian and Adriana left the table. Mother Fidelis tried to smooth over the tension by telling a funny incident from earlier in the day. Sister Immaculata and I persuaded her to give more details. As she did the three of us were uncontrollably laughing. *Are we really laughing this hard from the story or from pent-up tension during supper?*

Later I asked Sister Immaculata, "What's the matter with Sister Killian? I remember you held her in high esteem."

"Yes, when we were young missionaries before WWII, the people used to refer to Sister Killian as a woman without guile."

"So, what happened? Was it the war?"

"Indirectly. She couldn't get home to Wales during the war and by the time she returned both parents were dead. It's left her an embittered woman. It saddens me and I pray for her. I ask you not to judge her but to pray for her. We were once young like you are now, Sister Kathleen. We were also full of zeal and fervour."

I sympathized with Sister Immaculata's disappointment. She had the memory of what had been, but the person in front of her didn't resemble the treasured memory. "I'll try to be patient and understanding," I assured her.

A few nights later I was woken rudely from a dream by a man roaring, "Vaya de aca."

*Whose voice is this? It sounds violent. Is he speaking to the devil?* I knelt on my bed to peer out the small window above the headboard. I couldn't see anyone outside. My radio-alarm showed 2:10 a.m. The community room on the opposite side of the interior patio with its high-polished red floor was in darkness. I turned on my bedside lamp and slowed my racing heart.

Sister Killian spoke through my closed bedroom door, "Get dressed. There's a maternity case. I'll give you the details later."

My extremities wobbled from the roar that had woken me. I couldn't recall the dream but I knew it had been a wonderful dream. I dressed quickly in my white nurse's uniform and placed the white shoulder-length veil on top of my uncombed hair.

## Chapter Twenty-Four

## NORTHERN COASTAL BIRTHS

The cream-coloured station wagon idled. Sister Killian was in the driver's seat, tapping impatiently on the rear-view mirror. *She's annoyed I didn't come faster. She forgets she was fully dressed when she came to get me. Attending a birth should be joyful. But if she kills the joy I'll call her Killjoy.*

I seated myself in the front passenger seat, my maternity box on my lap. She glanced sideways at my shiny box and said, "You won't need that. I'll be doing the delivery."

She swung the wheel left and we skidded out of the loose gravel parking lot onto the paved road. The headlights split the blackness of the night. She sped through the narrow winding back streets. The rear of the station wagon swayed from side to side. I clung to my box like a child clings to a security blanket.

I saw no streetlights or street names. *If the town doesn't have electricity how come our convent does? How will we attend a birth with no lights in the house?*

The station wagon halted in front of a single-story wooden house with faded green paint. A man in a tattered thin poncho waved his arms. With one foot out the car, Sister Killian said,

"That's the husband. The patient is having her first baby. I'll attend to her and you'll attend to the baby." She closed the driver's door firmly and opened the rear door for her maternity bag.

*Killjoy doesn't call the woman or her husband by name? Her approach to a home birth is so impersonal. Mrs. Doherty and Mac were personable. I miss them.*

We entered the house and Sister Killian directed her high beam flashlight at the crude wood floor, scattering the cockroaches. This was a fishermen's house. Wealthy families owned the fishing fleets and lived in two-or three-storey houses. They hired the fishermen.

The man in the tattered poncho said, "Welcome to my house. Come this way."

I said to the expectant mother, "Buenos dias, Señora. I'm Sister Kathleen and this is Sister Killian."

"Buenos dias. I'm Maribel and my husband, Victor."

Our pleasantries annoyed Sister Killian. She said in English, "We're here to attend a delivery not to socialize."

She didn't speak Spanish to the couple. Instead, she used her own form of sign language. She patted the bed with the palm of her hand indicating Maribel was to lie down.

She said to me, "The fetal head is down in the pelvis. The heart is regular, strong at 128 beats per minute."

I translated this to Maribel even though I wasn't asked to translate. Sister Killian flicked the elastic on Maribel's panties and motioned for her to remove them. Maribel looked at me.

I put my hand on her shoulder and said in Spanish, "It's okay, Maribel. Sister will examine you to know when your baby will be born."

Maribel squeezed my fingers during the internal examination. Sister Killian estimated baby would be born in four or five hours.

In the seventies it wasn't customary in Perú for husbands to attend childbirth so Victor left. Maribel's mother stayed in the kitchen boiling water and making chicken soup.

Sister Killian said, "It's important in Perú for the new mother to drink a hot mug of chicken soup as soon as the placenta is expelled. The mother will spoon feed her daughter the soup."

Maribel was able to enjoy her mother's chicken soup shortly after 8:00 a.m. when her baby boy was born.

"It's customary for the grandmother to dress the newborn," Sister Killian told me.

"Thanks for telling me," I said. "I'll leave dressing baby to Maribel's mother."

After I had finished attending to the umbilical cord and bathing baby, I handed baby to his grandmother.

First, she removed the top cardboard box from the stack against the wooden wall. I wondered why there were so many boxes. They lined three bedroom walls, rising from the floor to the corrugated tin roof. From the box the grandmother removed clean well-pressed baby clothes, a baby shawl, and a long narrow strip of white cotton. *Ah, the boxes stand in for dressers and a wardrobe.* I watched her dress the infant, wrap him in the shawl, and tie the long narrow strip around him to restrict him from moving. Lastly, she tied a red string around the baby's wrist.

"This superstitious custom is to ward off 'El Mal de Ojo', the Evil Eye," Sister Killian said to me in English. "Red represents strength. They believe it'll protect the baby from strangers looking at him with a bad intention in their heart."

I made no comment to this explanation.

*I don't see a crib. I guess baby will sleep with his parents.*

It was like the grandmother read my thoughts. She reached for another box, emptied the clothes onto the foot of Maribel's bed, and lined the box with a white sheet. Baby was placed in this improvised crib after Maribel finished breast feeding him.

Victor was now permitted to enter the room. "Thank you for attending to my wife and son," he said.

Before Sister Killian left Maribel and Victor, she used her sign language to say we'd return in a few hours to check up on mother and baby.

I didn't return for Maribel's checkup because another woman started labour. "Sister Immaculata will drive you to this woman's house," Sister Killian said. "Examine her. I'll come when I finish my postnatal visits."

*Good. Finally, I'll get to speak with Sister Immaculata alone.*

In the station wagon I told her about being woken by a man screaming. "Did you hear a man screaming last night?"

"Father Al shouts if a fisherman knocks on his door instead of on our door when Sister Killian is needed for a maternity case."

"He better not wake me like that again," I replied. "Or I won't knock on his door, I'll break the door down."

Sister Immaculata smiled. "Don't let him get to you. It's not worth it. I think he's a mentally disturbed man."

"If he's mentally disturbed why the heck did his bishop allow him to start a mission in Perú?"

Sister tightened her lips. "Unfortunately, sometimes this is what some bishops and religious congregations do with their troubled clergy and sisters. Instead of getting them the help they need they send them to the foreign missions. Once in a mission country they move from place to place as no one can live with them. Father Al moved several times before our sisters accepted him."

Our conversation ended as we arrived at the expectant mother's home. "I'll come back in half an hour," Sister Immaculata said as she drove off.

The mother of the daughter in labour hugged me. "Welcome, Sister."

"Thank you, I'm Hermana Catalina."

Hugging is as much a way of life in Latino cultures as is loud music. The mother ushered me into the small bedroom where I met her daughter. Fela was chatty which told me she was in early labour. Shortly after I examined her to confirm my suspicion Sister Immaculata returned. She hugged the mother and daughter then took me aside. "Did you see the statue of Saint Martin de Porres on the porch table?"

"No. Why?"

"Because the statue is turned upside down."

We went to the porch and saw Saint Martin de Porres standing on his head with his broom pointed upwards. Lit candles encircled the statue on the table.

Legend has it that Saint Martin de Porres, a Peruvian Dominican Friar, collected left-over bread from the refectory and gave it to beggars outside the friary door. He swept away the crumbs with his broom. I asked the mother, "Why is Saint Martin de Porres on his head?"

Her explanation was simple and logical. "When I gave birth to my daughter she came bum first. It was a long painful labour. I want my daughter's baby to be born head first."

I smiled. "Señora, you can stand Saint Martin de Porres on his feet as your daughter's baby is coming head first."

"But you don't know this for certain."

"I better know it for certain." I said, tapping my fingers against the wardrobe. "The baby's head is as hard as this wardrobe."

She believed me and turned the statue of Saint Martin de Porres on his feet with his broom downwards.

"I'll bring Sister Killian back," Sister Immaculata said, and off she went again.

Once Sister Killian returned and satisfied herself all was well, she said, "I'm too tired to attend this birth. Sister Adriana will be with you shortly."

Throughout the day Fela's contractions got stronger and quicker. She laboured for seven hours before she was ready to push with her contractions. Her mother wiped Fela's brow between pushes and witnessed the baby's head crowning. With her final push, Fela gave birth to a healthy baby girl.

Chapter Twenty-Five

## THE FISH FACTORY

Father Al said, "Sister Kathleen, come sit on the veranda. I want to talk with you."

"Okay, I'll be there in five minutes."

I went to the washroom and placed a cold wet facecloth on the back of my neck. February and March are the hottest months in the southern hemisphere. The cold water both cooled and calmed me. *Don't react to whatever he says. Listen and take slow deep breaths.*

We sat in wicker rocking chairs facing the ocean. Sometimes from the veranda, if I was lucky, I'd see a pod of dolphins, sleek animals leaping from the water. When a ship appeared on the horizon, it brought deep-sea fish, like black cod, to the fishermen. They would paddle the waves on balsawood rafts to meet the ship. Each raft consisted of five six-foot balsa logs tightly strapped together. I was intrigued with the buoyancy of these rafts and how they'd line up alongside the ship like taxis outside an airport. Black cod which weighed 40 to 50 kilograms were tossed down onto the rafts. Each fisherman returned to the shore where a freezer truck waited to receive this exotic fish. The black cod was loaded into the freezer and transported to the capital to be eaten in elegant hotels by tourists, business folk and Lima's dignitaries. We who lived where the black cod swam never feasted on this oily fish delicacy.

"I want to talk to you about the fish factory next door. I made a deal with the manager. He provides us with electricity, I provide him with a registered nurse. You're the only RN as Sisters Killian and Adriana are midwives."

*Really? This is news to me. It explains why Sister Killian seems to resent me and belittle me whenever she has the opportunity. It also explains why we have electricity and the town doesn't.*

"I spoke with the factory manager this morning," Father Al continued, "and he has made a room available for you to use as a clinic for attending the factory employees. How would you feel about working in the fish factory?"

*Anything is better than working with Killjoy. Do I have a choice if I want to remain in Perú? The deal has been made. I'm just a pawn Father Al moves around for his benefit.*

"I don't know," I said. "I've never been in a factory of any kind."

"Then I'll drive you over to meet the manager and have a tour of the factory. But first there's another matter we need to discuss. Sisters Killian and Adriana use two rooms as a dispensary in a building by the church for their maternity work."

"Yes, I've been in there. They do prenatal care on certain days and attend to the sick on other days."

"That's correct. But El Ministerio de Salud, the Ministry of Health, came and inspected our dispensary. They asked for the name of the RN in charge of dispensing medications. To prevent the dispensary from being closed I gave your name to the minister. I've told the sisters from now on you'll be the only one to dispense medicines."

"How can I work in the dispensary and factory as well?"

Father Al said, "Easy. The dispensary is open from 8:00 a.m. to 1:00 p.m. Monday to Friday and the factory clinic will be two days a week from 3:00 p.m. to 6:00 p.m. You and the manager can decide which two days will be best for both of you. He'll drive you to and from the factory."

On my tour of the factory I saw women in knee-high rubber boots washing fish in long deep troughs. They stood on wooden crates above wet slippery concrete floors. In the freezer room men stored fish in boxes. The below-zero temperature transformed my uniform into a crisp crinoline. These were the working conditions of the employees I'd treat. The manager used a handheld microphone to announce to his employees: "This is our nurse, Hermana Catalina."

I waved and mouthed, "Hola" to the sea of smiling faces.

To my surprise, I felt at home. My work in the factory came to be not only my refuge from Sister Killian but a place I looked forward to working every Tuesday and Thursday afternoon. Ricardo, the manager, was a cheerful chubby man in his forties. The employees respected him as he treated them well. Occasionally he'd allow them to take left-over fish home.

After a few weeks I knew most of the employees by name. I'd send for women to come to see me to give them a break from standing by the troughs. They deposited small puddles on the concrete floor of the one-room clinic, which smelled of fish. I treated arthritis in the knees, hips and hands. "Rub this anti-inflammatory cream on your swollen joint and take this anti-inflammatory tablet with your night meal. Let me know if the medicine helps you."

In the winter months many had respiratory infections but continued to work. Few could afford an unpaid sick day. Pregnant women weren't permitted to clean fish. I never knew if there was a superstitious belief that pregnancy affected the fish or if management didn't want the woman to slip on the wet floors. Hence a woman concealed her pregnancy under the heavy rubber apron for as long as she could.

These employees were my patients but soon became my friends. Not personal friends with whom I confided, but friends who teased me when I didn't use the correct Spanish word or didn't understand a colloquial expression. We laughed readily which I didn't do with either Sister Killian or Sister Adriana. I wasn't lonely in the factory.

I was on my guard in the dispensary. Sister Killian stormed in on her way to the biffy in the back room several times a morning. She was full of complaints. "The medicine bottles aren't in a straight row on the shelves. How do you expect to find a medicine?"

I never responded.

Another repetitive criticism was, "There are too many unwashed empty bottles in the sink. When do you plan on washing them? Or do you?"

I learned to ignore her presence and focus on my patients.

※ ※ ※

EVERYONE IN THE WAITING ROOM took a number and waited their turn. One morning when I opened the waiting room door, I saw a mother cradling a very sick-looking baby in her arms. I indicated for her to come forward into the dispensary. No one objected.

"Señora, how old is your baby?"

"Five months."

After taking his temperature and listening to his lungs I gave her pediatric Tylenol drops for his fever and a pediatric antibiotic for his acute bronchitis. "Señora, medicines alone won't cure your baby's infection. The air around baby's crib has to be moist to help baby breathe easier. I need you to place a pan of water near the crib." *Don't tell her to put the water in a pot or bowl because she needs the pot for cooking and the bowl for soup or rice.* "Señora, it isn't important what you use to hold the water. You can use a potty." *Every home has several potties as there's no running water in their houses.* "What is important is for the water to moisten the air. Do you understand what I'm asking you to do, Señora?"

"Sí, Hermana."

*Don't tell her to put the potty on a table or chair as she may not have either.* I said, "Put the potty on the floor. Señora, do you have any questions?"

"Sí. You told me to put the potty on the floor. I don't have a floor. I have stamped dirt in my house."

"This is fine. Put the potty on the stamped dirt. What is important is to keep the air near baby's crib moist. I'll come and see your baby later this afternoon."

I've never forgotten this humble and truthful mother. She reminded me to live without pretense. Her baby overcame the bout of bronchitis in the subsequent weeks and thrived.

## Chapter Twenty-Six

## The DISPENSARY

Expectant mothers had to sit in the waiting room with the sick if they didn't attend the pre-natal day with Sisters Killian and Adriana. When Rosa came into the dispensary room, I asked her, "How may I help you?"

"I'm four months pregnant." She looked radiant.

"That's nice. Is it your first pregnancy?"

"Yes, Sister, it's my first pregnancy."

After checking her blood pressure, pulse and temperature, I asked her to lie on the examination table. I drew the curtain while I examined her abdomen. "If I can feel your uterus above the pubic bone then I'll agree with you that you're four months pregnant." She smiled.

I said, "You're correct. You're four months pregnant."

In a reserved voice she said, "Sister, I have a problem."

"What is your problem?"

She hesitated. "Tengo una solitaria."

I had never heard this word 'solitaria' and took it for 'soltera'. Trying to console her, I said, "Many women become wonderful single mothers."

"But, Sister, you don't understand. I want to get rid of it."

*She knows we're Catholic sisters. Why has she come to us wanting an abortion?* Instead of asking this I said, "You know sometimes the immediate solution isn't always the best solution."

She frowned. "But I got rid of one before."

*If she has had one abortion, why didn't she use birth control pills to prevent another pregnancy? She has lied to me. She told me this was her first pregnancy.* Now I felt no compassion towards her. *Kathleen, take a deep breath and don't judge her. How would Jesus treat this woman?* I calmed myself and asked, "Do your parents know?"

Puzzled with this question she said, "Sister, I'm married."

Stunned. I asked, "What was the word you used that sounded like 'soltera'?"

"Solitaria. A worm."

"A worm?"

"Yes, a big long worm." She stretched her hands wide apart to demonstrate how long.

*Oh, no, she's got a tape worm and is pregnant.* Needless to say I've never forgotten that word!

"Señora Rosa, I can't give you medicine to purge the tapeworm as it'd probably cause you to lose your baby."

"Oh no, my husband and I want this baby."

"What I'll do is increase your vitamins and iron intake. You'll need to eat more vegetables and avoid sweets." I knew Rosa and her husband weren't financially poor like most of my patients. "When you're eight months pregnant you'll need to be hospitalized for treatment. They'll want to keep you for a few days after the treatment, to monitor baby. In the interim you may come here for your prenatal care."

"Thank you, Sister."

When I told Sisters Killian and Adriana about Rosa's condition,

Sister Adriana said, "Tapeworms come from ceviche made from fish caught in the harbour. Ceviche is marinated raw fish. Unless it's made from deep-sea fish it has a high risk of being infested with tapeworms or other species of worms."

"Scary," I said. "I see the locals eating ceviche in the plaza. It looks so good."

"Most of the children have parasites. Be aware of this when you're treating them in the dispensary. They present with anaemia or with respiratory infections but the underlying cause is parasites."

"Thanks for telling me. I'll be conscious of this when treating the children."

*Today they talk like they're okay with me being the only one permitted to dispense medicines. A few months ago they resented this change. Is it because now that I'm stuck in the dispensary, they've got a monopoly on maternity cases? Maybe I need to let them know I want to attend deliveries.*

"You know I could do deliveries Monday, Wednesday, and Friday afternoons as well as on weekends and at night."

Sister Adriana walked away as she always did when she didn't want to listen to something.

Sister Killian said, "Every time we've a delivery you're in chapel praying. Or in your room playing your guitar. During the night we come and go but you never get up. You don't show much interest in delivering babies."

"That's not fair. I feel you don't want me doing deliveries. I get the impression you and Sister Adriana are boycotting me, Sister Killian."

"I don't have time for this nonsense. If you're not happy, tell Father Al. He's the one who put you in charge of the dispensary and work in the factory." With those words she retreated to her sleeping quarters.

*Kathleen, hang in. Remember how much love the Peruvian people show you every day. You're here for them. Don't let Killjoy take that from you.*

※ ※ ※

THE NEXT DAY WHEN I closed the padlock on the dispensary door at 1:00 p.m. a short man ran by me hysterically crying, "Marietta esta dando luz." (Marietta is giving light... meaning *birth*).

Sister Killian shouted from the idling station wagon, "RUN! Through the passageway beside the church. RUN. I'll bring the maternity bag." I was in Marietta's house within a minute, but couldn't see until my eyes adjusted from the bright sun to the dim room. Then... what I saw was terrifying.

Marietta lay across the bed with her feet planted on the edge. Between her flabby thighs hung a puny half-born baby. The baby's legs and bum were hanging in midair with the thin umbilical cord dangling alongside the bony legs. In horror I reached for the baby with my bare hands to deliver the upper portion of baby's body and head. On complete expulsion from the womb baby was wet, slimy, cold and lifeless. By the time Sister Killian arrived with the maternity bag, I had the baby wrapped in the bed sheet and was performing mouth-to-mouth resuscitation. I quickly learned that what I had read in midwifery textbooks – 'only blow with the air in your cheeks' – was written by a midwife who had no experience of mouth-to-mouth resuscitation in a newborn. Surprisingly I had to blow with air from my lungs before I saw the baby's chest elevate.

I grabbed a plastic mucus extractor from Sister Killian's maternity bag, and cleaned baby's airways but still there was no sign of life. I drew up Coramine (today known as Nikethamide) into a glass syringe and jabbed the needle into baby's thigh. Sister

Killian cut the umbilical cord and was delivering the placenta when Marietta started haemorrhaging.

Sister Killian yelled at me in a high-pitched voice, "Leave the baby. Come help me."

This was Marietta's seventh pregnancy. We sisters had begged her to go to hospital for her prenatal care and delivery. She needed to have an ultrasound to diagnose how many months pregnant she was and to check the presentation of the fetus. We were unable to determine either due to her obesity and lax abdominal muscles. But Marietta was too laid back to take anything we said seriously. She'd always laugh and say, "I've delivered six babies at home. I know what to expect."

As I moved away from the presumably dead baby boy to help with Marietta I either heard a feeble cry or saw the baby's chest move. To this day, I don't know what happened. But I exclaimed, "THE BABY IS ALIVE!"

Sister Killian who now had the bleeding under control shouted, "Go back to the baby."

I attended to the umbilical cord and massaged baby's extremities while keeping him on his left side. Finally, baby gave a strong cry and regained muscle tone. He no longer felt like a wet flimsy dishcloth. I estimated his prematurity was equivalent to 35-weeks' gestation (full term being 40 weeks). I wrapped baby in a dirty garment I found hanging on a nail and handed him to his mother. Marietta didn't delay in putting him to her breast. Cleanliness in this emergency took back seat to survival.

Later, Sister Killian crudely said, "Pigs thrive in the muck."

I preferred to believe Marietta's babies thrived on parental love and breast milk.

By the fourth postnatal day, baby's injection site appeared red, warm to the touch and swollen. In my panic to save his life I had contaminated the needle. I looked at Marietta. "I'm sorry about this abscess. It's my fault." I handed her a bottle and said, "You'll have to give him this oral antibiotic every twelve hours for five days."

"No problem," Marietta said in her laid-back fashion. "He's alive and for that I'm grateful to God and to you."

"Marietta, give these drops to baby for fever or if you think he has pain. Please don't touch the abscess. I'll attend to it when it's mature." I had learned to wait until a white speck appeared in the centre of the abscess before piercing it.

There's no medical explanation for why this premature baby hanging from the birth canal in midair lived and had no brain damage in spite of the fact he received no oxygen. And no explanation for why he rapidly gained weight with a leg abscess. I learned from this maternity case there's no logical explanation for who lives and who dies. It was this baby's time to live.

Chapter Twenty-Seven

## REMEMBRANCE

On Saturday, June 29th 1975, the early morning sun danced on the sparkling ocean waves for La Fiesta de San Pedro. Although it was winter in Perú, the harbour water was warm due to the Humboldt and El Niño currents.

For a month before the feast of Saint Peter I watched women sitting on the sandy shore making colourful streamers and banners for their husbands and sons to attach to the frame of their fishing rowboats. The town buzzed with excitement in anticipation of the celebrations that would take place on the day.

Even Sister Killian wasn't as grumpy as usual amidst these festive preparations. She said, "In the week of the 29th our local population will swell with visitors from everywhere. Both sides of the main road will be lined with kiosks selling food and souvenir trinkets."

"Will we be able to drive the main road to attend the dispensary or a maternity case?"

"Yes, because the civil guards keep traffic moving and the freezer trucks aren't permitted to park."

"That's good. Because they're so huge that I feel unsafe walking by them."

"According to our prenatal book no woman is due to give birth during this year's week of festivities," Sister Killian stated. "For the past two celebrations of this feast we were too busy to have any fun."

Each evening of that week Mother Fidelus, Sister Immaculata and I walked with the tourists. We enjoyed checking out the various kiosks. Some sold earthenware pottery, others hand-knitted llama gloves, sweaters and scarves as well as alpaca ponchos. The kiosks were interesting but noisy due to the generators behind them. Some kiosks cranked up music to camouflage the unwanted buzz.

Closer to the plaza where the old adobe brick church faced the ocean were the food stalls. There was a stand with hot donuts dipped in caramel sauce, a cotton candy stall and, the most popular of all, a stall for dishes of ceviche and lobster.

The mood was definitely upbeat and I loved it. *This is so much better than the dark isolated streets I've experienced up until now. I wish we had streetlights and it was lively like this all the time.*

"What is that high wooden tower at the far end of the harbour?" I asked. "I haven't seen it there before."

"Luckily Father Al is away," said Sister Immaculata. "He always fumes when he sees the fireworks structure. It costs thousands of soles but it's how Peruvians honour their patron saint."

Mother Fidelus added, "It reminds me of how we celebrate in Switzerland. Wait until you see how magnificent and magical the sky will look, Sister Kathleen, when these fireworks are set off on Friday evening."

It was spectacular to witness the brilliant multicoloured fireworks shooting high into the night sky, hearing one sizzle out then the next explode into an enormous display of rainbow proportions. It dazzled my eyes and heart with sheer delight almost as much as watching the gleeful children running around in delirious excitement.

※ ※ ※

The four-foot plaster statue of Saint Peter in his fishing boat mounted on a wooden platform remained in the centre aisle of the church overnight. In the morning Sister Immaculata celebrated a para-liturgical service with scripture readings and prayers before she sprinkled holy water on Saint Peter and laid the remembrance wreath at his feet.

The church was too small to accommodate the musicians, so they stood on the steps playing their drums, horns, flutes and zampoñas. When the service ended at 10:00 a.m. the ceremonial music helped the fishermen balance the arms of the platform on their shoulders while they carried Saint Peter upright in his boat. The congregation threw petals onto the statue and pathway as Saint Peter was led into the water on a balsa raft before being lifted onto a large fishing boat in deep water. The band continued playing as they too boarded the boat and stood behind the statue.

"Sister Kathleen," Sister Killian said. "Since this is your first year here, we think you should be the one to go out to the high sea in the boat with Saint Peter and the band. It's customary that a priest or sister accompany the fishermen. They'll throw the remembrance wreath overboard for all who have died at sea."

"I don't know how to swim. Are there life-jackets on the boat?"

"I doubt it. Don't worry. You'll be fine."

So I waded in and climbed on board a rowboat which took me to the big fishing boat. The fishermen hoisted me up from the rowboat onto their boat. With my feet apart on the wet wooden planks I balanced myself and watched the hundreds of men, women and children on the shore. They were getting into over-crowded rowboats decorated with the colourful streamers and banners the women had made in anticipation of this day. Finally, after an hour of boarding, the overcrowded boats rowed away from the harbour and were in procession behind Saint Peter. I counted about fifteen with mostly women and girls sitting on both sides wearing no lifejackets and men and boys standing in the centre. *I've never seen so many people packed into a rowboat. I guess Peruvian fishermen and their families are at home on the high sea.*

I remained in the helm of the engine-powered boat watching the waves rippling away. It was mesmerizing. When we were in the deep water the captain quieted the engine so the boat was stationary. Then he signalled with his arm for the band to stop playing. Into the white-capped waves the captain threw the large wreath with red poppies attached in the shape of little crosses overboard. Everyone made the sign of the cross and watched in silence until the wreath was no longer visible. The band started playing again.

The engine quickly propelled the boat into a homeward turn. But the powerful wake rocked some of the over-crowded rowboats causing them to capsize. I saw women and children in the water and men jumping from their boats. For a second, I thought they'd jumped in for a swim as I was so used to seeing people swimming in the harbour. Only when I saw the alarmed faces of the captain and his crew did I realize these adults and children were fighting for their lives. A few over-turned rowboats were bobbing on top of the high waves. Our boat continued moving slowly toward the shore away from the people struggling in the water. And the band continued to play.

"Why are we leaving them?" I shouted to the captain. "We need to help them! Don't we have something to throw to them?"

"Our boat is increasing the strength of the waves," the captain replied. "We have to move slowly away to prevent more rocking of these shallow boats too near to our vessel."

I can still feel the helplessness I felt that day in the helm of the boat with the loud music playing and our boat moving farther and farther from the bodies in the water. *I'm a nurse I should be helping not abandoning people in need. But I'm of no use... I can't swim.*

Fishermen continued to dive into the water trying to save the women and children. As our boat neared the shore I saw the horrified faces of Mother Fidelus and Sisters Immaculata, Killian and Adriana amidst the wailing crowd.

Now with my shaking legs on the beach and tears running down my face I blurted out in English to the sisters, "The captain refused to stay. He said, 'Our boat is increasing the waves.'"

"He was correct," Sister Killian said. "It was a hard decision for him to make as a fisherman."

"And the band kept playing like nothing was wrong."

"Sister Kathleen, let's go back to the convent," Mother Fidelus suggested.

She made me tea and added a teaspoon of brandy and some honey. After I warmed up and stopped shaking, we went to chapel and prayed *The Lord is My Shepherd* together. Then she left me alone with the Lord.

That evening and every evening for the next week the incoming tide deposited water-logged purple bodies on the beaches. The longer it took for a body to be washed up the more the body was mutilated. The stench was overpowering. The fishermen's common words were: "The ocean always gives up her dead. We just have to wait."

Bodies were washed up on beaches in adjacent cities. Everyone in the department of Piura knew of our tragedy and brought our loved ones back to us. Sister Immaculata held a nightly vigil in the church, which remained open 24-7 for people to grieve alone and together.

Readers, by the time this book is published and in your hands it will be the 50th anniversary of those who died at sea while celebrating their patron saint. I remember them. And I honour all fishermen worldwide who risk their lives to bring us fish.

Chapter Twenty-Eight

## EVERY FIVE WEEKS

A community of American sisters lived two hours north of us in a large city with a general hospital, schools, a large indoor market, a post office and a football stadium. The sisters ran a well-equipped maternity hospital. Their convent was a two-storey building that could accommodate visitors. They invited our sisters, one at a time, to spend a weekend with them. We welcomed the opportunity. Our fishing town wasn't only without electricity, it also lacked a post office and a market. Although we boasted about our fresh catches of lobster and other exotic fish, a fish factory, elementary and secondary schools, we were only a small community.

While in the larger city we sisters collected our mail from the central post office and mailed letters home. In the indoor market we bought papaya, mango, guava, pineapple, avocado and other fresh vegetables. What I appreciated most about being in the larger city was walking on grass in the parks. Our town was a barren wasteland apart from our beaches.

I was happy to receive letters from my mother and Bonnie, but elated when I saw Drew's blue airmail envelope. I treasured his letters and read them several times, often while sitting on top of a huge jagged rock by the sea. My tears mingled with the ocean mist on my face. Sometimes I stared at his handwriting trying to feel his presence. Other times I kissed the paper and held it close to my heart. Drew's letters reminded me that I was loved, valued and respected... what I didn't feel with Sisters Killian and Adriana. I wrote back to him during my weekends off, and mailed my letters before returning.

※ ※ ※

THE MONTH OF AUGUST PROVED to be the most fun-loving month I had experienced in our northern convent. An East Indian sister lived with us for three-weeks while on vacation from nursing school in London, England. Sister Blessica was 28 years of age, like myself. We immediately became best friends and giggled often during meals – to the distress of Sister Killian and the amusement of Mother Fidelus and Sister Immaculata.

I confined to her, "I don't like to attend births with Sister Killian as I witnessed her slapping the women's thighs."

Sister Blessica's eyebrows arched, "Why would she slap the labouring mother?"

"Because that is just how she is. I think sometimes she'd like to slap me too!"

"This is shocking for me to hear. Are you going to stay here?"

"I don't have too many options since this is our only mission in Perú and I love the Peruvian culture and people."

"Yeah, you're in a tough situation. Maybe by abiding your time things will work out for you."

"I sure hope so. I just don't want the Peruvian people to think this is how all sisters behave. Anyways, thanks for listening. I needed to share this."

※ ※ ※

One afternoon when Sister Blessica and I had the house to ourselves I suggested, "Why don't we bake a cake?"

She asked, "Do you think Mother Fidelus would mind as normally she bakes the cakes?"

"Yes, I know… but her cakes are always so heavy."

"Maybe she doesn't sift the flour."

"I don't know." I confessed. "I just think it would be a nice change for us to bake one."

"Okay. Let's do it."

We followed the recipe for baking a cake and all looked fine. When I opened the kitchen counter drawer, beside the stove, to retrieve the oven mitts I saw a small package of yeast and asked, "Sister Blessica, what do you think if we sprinkle some yeast into our cake batter? Maybe Mother's cakes are so heavy because she doesn't use yeast."

"Yeah, sounds good to me."

We sprinkled the yeast on top of the batter then stirred it into the mixture before placing the cake tin on the oven rack. Soon the aroma filled the small kitchen. Periodically we opened the oven door a crack to peek at our enterprise. To our joy the cake had risen 5 inches.

When the allotted baking time was up, we removed the cake tin from the oven and gloated over our achievement. As soon as the cake cooled, we eagerly sliced into the cake which caused the hard roof to collapse! There was literally a 5-inch hollow space.

In panic I said, "We have to get rid of this before the sisters return."

"What can we do to hide it?"

"We'll go down the concrete stairs in the retainer wall to the waterfront and feed the cake to the seabirds."

"Good idea. And let's keep the external kitchen door open and the ceiling fan on while we're feeding the seabirds."

"Smart thinking."

When the sisters returned no one made any comment or asked if we had been baking. Our small cake disaster went unnoticed. A few days later Sister Blessica left to return to her nursing program in England.

※ ※ ※

ON A SATURDAY MORNING WHEN Sister Adriana was on her weekend off, Sister Killian yelled, "Sister Kathleen, there's an emergency delivery."

Once we were in the station wagon, I watched her face go from pale to grey. "A 16-year-old in her first pregnancy is in advanced labour. I'm suspecting that the baby is breech. The partera (an untrained midwife) stayed with her overnight. An hour ago, the girl's water broke and the partera didn't feel a head... so she came for us."

"Oh my God. Let's hope the umbilical cord hasn't slipped down. We're transporting her to hospital for a C-Section... right?"

"No. The motion of the car will increase the rate of contractions. She'll deliver en route and we'll possibly lose mother and baby. It's almost a given we'll lose the baby. My goal is to save this teenager."

I entered the small dark windowless bedroom with its stamped-dirt floor and stopped in shock. The mother was cuddling her teenage daughter who yelled uncontrollably through each contraction. I knew this family. The daughter was Carmelita.

Sister Killian said, "I'll do the delivery. You take care of baby. You're better at resuscitation."

Her internal examination confirmed a breech presentation. It was a frank breech presentation, where the buttocks acted like a plug preventing the umbilical cord from slipping out. Baby's legs were straight up with the feet under the chin. I listened to baby's heart with the metal trumpet. It was strong and regular.

"She's fully dilated and needs to push with her contractions," Sister Killian said.

I told the mother, "You need to stop cuddling Carmelita. She needs to push with her contractions."

The mother continued to hold Carmelita and allow her to scream through a contraction. I knew that this was an increasingly dangerous situation. So, I took the mother by the hand and led her into the kitchen. Then I did a quick about-turn and closed and latched the bedroom door. Before the next contraction started, I bluntly explained to Carmelita, "If you scream through your contractions instead of taking a deep breath and pushing, you'll cause the death of your baby. We can do nothing to save your baby until the head is born. Right now we can only watch. You're the only person who can save your baby. I'll tell you when to take a deep breath and when to push."

Carmelita followed my instructions. She didn't scream again. She saved her baby's life.

She enjoyed her mother's chicken soup while I bathed the baby. Her mother hugged me and thanked Sister Killian.

"You're fortunate your partera sent for us," I said. "She too needs to be thanked."

Both Carmelita and her mother promised me they'd thank the partera.

In Perú in the late seventies fetal and maternal mortality rates were high. This delivery once more confirmed my desire to teach. *I want to use this maternity case as a great example of how parteras and professionally trained people can work together. This partera recognized an abnormality and sent for help before it was too late. I want to teach parteras how to recognize the need for professional help even earlier in the labour. I could teach them the dangers of turning a baby during pregnancy, and the dangers of binding a newborn tightly to prevent movement. I can help lower these death rates if I'm permitted to teach these and other preventative methods.*

On our return drive to the convent Sister Killian, who was no longer a pale shade of grey, said, "I'm sure you must miss Sister Blessica." Then she quickly added, "Now you have no one to feed the seabirds with."

Stunned, I didn't respond. I never did find out how she knew about our botched cake incident.

## Chapter Twenty-Nine

## ANGELS FROM THE WOMB

Sister Immaculata came to the fish factory. "Sister Kathleen, I have to drive an expectant mother who is seven months pregnant to the private mining hospital. She's in early labour at 4 centimetres dilation. Baby's heart is strong and regular. Sisters Killian and Adriana think it's safer for her to deliver in hospital."

"I agree," I said. Then laughed. "Who cares if I agree, eh?"

Sister Immaculata raised her blue eyes. "Sister Kathleen, could you leave the clinic and come with me?"

"Yes, of course I'll come with you. It's near closing time and the employees are ready to call it a day."

I locked the clinic door and sat in the front passenger seat of the station wagon. The expectant mother was lying down in the back. "Greetings," I said. "I'm Sister Kathleen."

"I'm Philomena."

Sister Immaculata started the engine. I checked with her, "We do have maternity bags with us, eh?"

"Yes. They're at Philomena's feet."

"Okay." Turning to Philomena I asked, "This is your first pregnancy?"

"No, it's my third."

As we drove, I said to Sister Immaculata in English, "She could deliver en route."

"That's why we aren't going to the American sisters' hospital two hours away. The private mining hospital is only twenty minutes away and they have to accept emergency cases by law. We'll be fine."

"I sure hope so."

Philomena's contractions were well spaced at ten- and twelve-minute intervals. We were pretty sure we'd be at the hospital before her cervix was 6 centimetres dilated.

At the hospital Sister Immaculata told the security guard, "We've a mother in labour." He raised the metal arm barrier.

The Peruvian emergency room doctor came to the station wagon. Sister Immaculata told him through her open window what was happening. He didn't even look at our patient. "I think you've time to go to the American sisters' hospital," he said.

We were aghast. But there was nothing we could do or say to make him accept our patient.

Sister Immaculata turned the station wagon around and we headed up the hills. About half an hour later Philomena's contractions became strong and swift. She said, "I need to push."

Sister Immaculata couldn't stop on the winding, narrow hilly road for another ten minutes. Philomena pushed her baby from her womb.

When we were able to stop, I got out and opened the rear door. The small delicate premature baby's body lay lifeless on the blanket. Philomena was sobbing. "My baby hasn't cried."

I put the stethoscope on baby's chest even though I knew that her spirit had left her body. Looking at Philomena with tear-filled eyes I said, "I'm sorry."

With shaking hands and blurry eyes, I delivered the placenta while Sister Immaculata cradled Philomena.

When Sister Immaculata started up the motor of the station wagon I said, "We aren't going to the American sisters' hospital. We're returning to the private mining hospital."

Seeing my distress she agreed. This time we parked outside the emergency room and turned off the engine. I got out of the station wagon and pushed open the emergency swing doors. *I'll puff up this doctor's ego and then invite him to come out to meet our patient.*

"Doctor, you have much more training and knowledge than I have. And probably a lot more maternity experience too. Would you come and meet my patient and give me your opinion?"

With expanded chest and a broad smile, he walked outside. He accompanied me to the rear door of the station wagon. I opened the door and unwrapped the deceased baby. "This baby was alive when we brought this mother to you an hour ago. Live with the death of this baby on your conscience for the rest of your life."

He said nothing. He turned and walked back inside and we drove home.

The next day baby was buried in a shoebox in Philomena and Rolando's backyard. We sisters attended the burial. I cried continuously, holding hands with Philomena and Rolando. Sister Immaculata sprinkled holy water and said a prayer. She intoned a few traditional Lenten hymns.

The sons helped their father hammer and plant a white cross with their baby sister's name and date of birth on it. They named her Angelita.

※ ※ ※

WE MIDWIVES NOTICED THERE WERE always more births on a full-moon night. *Does the full moon's energy affect the waters around baby like it affects the ocean waves?* If we looked out to sea on a full-moon night we'd see a bright green streak shooting through the crashing waves. It was magical. Sister Killian told me, "The bright green streak is due to phosphorus. It's the energy of the full moon on the water."

"Like magnetic energy?"

"I guess."

Sisters Killian and Adriana attended two births one full-moon night and were called to a third woman in labour at 7:15 a.m.

"Sister Kathleen," Sister Killian said, "you'll have to go visit this woman. I don't know anything about her. She's not one of our prenatal women. Apparently, she came here last evening. No one knows her or where she came from. I'm told it's her first pregnancy. Examine her and I'll come as soon as Sister Adriana and I finish our postnatal visits."

I entered the two-room house. The expectant woman was pacing in the bedroom. The type of pacing a woman does before she stops and pushes. The woman who owned the house said, "I don't know who she is but I've offered her my house to give birth."

I gently asked the expectant mother to lie on the bed. The second her buttocks were lowered a huge gush of water deposited the umbilical cord on the mattress. Baby was in the breech presentation. "Help me move her sideways," I said to the owner.

Seconds later baby was born up to the armpits. I had a towel around baby's body and could feel its chubby legs wiggling. But the woman's contractions stopped.

I said, "Push."

She tried but baby didn't descend. The woman never had another contraction. Gradually the wiggling ceased and was replaced by a cold limp weight beneath the towel.

Sister Killian arrived and sprang into action. She pressed on the abdomen and told mother to push. I did an episiotomy to release the shoulders and delivered the deceased baby boy. The woman lay motionless. She knew her baby was dead yet didn't cry or ask to cradle him. That is how we left her. As soon as she was well enough to walk, she left our fishing town and was never heard from again. To this day, whenever there's a full moon, I remember this woman and her baby.

Chapter Thirty

## THE DECIDING FACTOR

Did stress cause the swelling in my right armpit? Did God permit my lymph nodes to swell? Maybe it was both or neither. I consulted a physician who diagnosed a small lump in my right breast. *Good. This provides me with a legitimate excuse for taking a medical leave of absence. If I had taken a stress leave of absence, I'd have received blame and judgement. Now I'll receive understanding and sympathy. Strange how that works, sympathy for physical sickness but judgement for emotional sickness.*

I shared the physician's finding with Mother Fidelis, who said, "I'm sorry, Sister. I'll contact Mother General and arrange for you to go to England as soon as possible."

"Thank you, Mother."

That evening Sister Immaculata came to sit with me on the veranda. In her caring manner she said, "How come you look so serious?"

After I told her, she frowned and asked, "How long have you had this?"

"Three months ago, I noticed discomfort when I raised my arm to get bottles off the top shelf. I assumed it was muscular. Then a few weeks ago swelling started in my armpit. It wakes me at night if I lie on my right side."

"I'm sorry. I hope it's nothing serious."

"I hope not."

Later when I told Sisters Killian and Adriana, Sister Adriana expressed concern and said, "Oh, I'm sorry. It'll be good to have a biopsy and know what's going on. In the meantime, try not to worry and get some extra rest."

Sister Killian merely rolled her eyes. "Young sisters only come to the missions for a cup of tea," she said as she walked away. Normally, a sister didn't return home for four years. I'd only been in the mission eighteen months.

Mother Fidelis came to the dispensary a few days later and said, "Sister Kathleen, here's your plane tickets. You'll fly to Lima tomorrow and there you will pick up your salida (the required document for leaving the country) and leave the next day for England."

"Thank you, Mother. I'm grateful for your help and support."

Missionary sisters were held in high esteem by physicians in England and given priority when seeking treatment. I was admitted to hospital the same week I arrived in Manchester. I had a private room. Around 9:00 p.m. there was a knock at the door. I presumed it was a nurse or an intern doctor.

"Come in."

The door opened and a tall thin priest in a grey suit and Roman collar entered. "Are you Sister Kathleen?"

"Yes?" I felt embarrassed in my nightie.

He introduced himself as the hospital chaplain. "I'm told you're having surgery tomorrow morning, Sister. Would you like the Sacrament of the Sick?"

Taken aback, I said, "No, I'm not dying."

He laughed. "Since Vatican II the Sacrament of the Sick is no longer reserved for the dying. It's a sacrament for healing."

"Well okay, I sure need healing. I've come from a stressful situation."

When he finished anointing me, I felt spiritually renewed and thanked him for coming. He wished me well and left the room.

The next morning the surgeon removed the lump which proved to be benign. For the next two weeks I had a lovely recovery time in the convent with my old friends: Mother Stephanie, Sister Joseph, Sister Thomas Francis and Sister Ursula. I delayed booking my return flight to Perú for another week. I wasn't eager to return to Father Al's nocturnal screams or to listen to Sister Killian's complaints.

On a Sunday afternoon two days before my departure, I phoned Father Drew. When I said, "Hello," he reacted excitedly. "Is that you, Katie?"

His voice sent a surge of affection through the centre of my body. My heart raced and my cheeks burned.

"Where are you?" he asked quickly.

"I'm here in Manchester at our convent. I had minor surgery two weeks ago and will be flying back to Perú on Tuesday."

"Can I see you tonight? I have an evening Mass at 5:00 but we could go for a drive afterwards."

"Yes. I'd love that."

"I'll pick you up at your convent at 7:00. How I'm looking forward to seeing *YOU*."

It was a warm summer evening when we drove to the manmade lake in the countryside. Drew parked the car to face the lake and we sat staring silently into each other's eyes, totally present to one another. I felt his hand tuck itself around the nape of my neck. I leaned my shoulder against the passenger seat. Our lips touched tenderly and re-touched before sealing together in a long enduring kiss. Drew's lips moved to kiss my cheek, then he took my hand, "Katie, if you weren't who you are and I wasn't who I am, would you marry me?"

"If this is a proposal," I teased, "I hope you can do better than that!"

"Oh, Katie, I love you. You're crazy. You know what I mean. If you weren't a nun and I weren't a priest, would you marry me?"

"Yes. Of course, I'd marry you."

We kissed, we embraced, and we kissed again. We left the car and walked hand-in-hand under a crimson sunset by the lake.

"Our love is not a possessive love," Drew said. "We choose to let each other live our dedicated religious lives separately." After a few seconds he added, "I still hope we'll have a married priesthood though."

"You're right, Drew. We're each dedicated to our religious commitments first and foremost. You're a great parish priest. I see how the parishioners love you and look to you for guidance. And I'm the fortunate missionary sister whose life is enriched with hugs from my Peruvian friends, in spite of their dehumanizing living conditions."

The remainder of our walk passed in silence as did our drive back to the convent.

I choked back tears as we embraced and said good-bye inside the convent alcove, but one salty tear rolled down the side of my face. I went straight to my room to allow myself to cry into my pillow.

*Jesus, I'm grateful you gave Drew and me this unexpected reunion. My breast scar will be my lifetime reminder of this treasured moment we shared in your presence. Amen.*

※ ※ ※

When I returned to our convent by the sea in northern Perú, Father Al was on a three-month sabbatical in Rome. Mother Fidelis and Sister Immaculata welcomed me with a buffet lunch on the veranda.

After lunch I requested to speak with Mother Fidelis.

"In England, I spoke with some nurses from the hospital where I trained. They highly encouraged me to get a Peruvian RN license if I'm going to continue dispensing medications. You see, Mother, they explained to me that the British Nursing Association won't defend me if anything goes wrong when I'm working here illegally without a Peruvian nursing license."

Mother said, "I understand, Sister Kathleen."

"Would I be able to go to Lima next week to start the paperwork?"

"I can't see why not. You may go to get your Peruvian license with my blessing."

With that settled, I shared the news with Sisters Immaculata, Killian and Adriana.

Sister Immaculata said, "That'll be a lot of hard work doing it in Spanish but I'm sure you'll do well with your strong determination to do the right thing."

Sisters Killian and Adriana as a team made no comment. A week later Mother Fidelis and Sister Immaculata again said their good-byes to me and I boarded the long-distance bus for Lima.

# PART IV

## NEAR THE CHILEAN BORDER

Chapter Thirty-One

## LIVING IN THE CAPITAL

Sisters owned large convents in Lima prior to Vatican II and ran private boarding schools for affluent Peruvian families. But with sisters leaving the order and the increasing number at retirement age, the remaining sisters decided to rent rooms to visiting sisters from other congregations. When I arrived unannounced, I was given a room, offered a hot shower, invited to community prayer, and to an evening meal. It was wonderful. Visiting sisters nicknamed the convent the Nuns' Hotel.

A Maltese sister, Sister Azalea, befriended me. "When I came with our sisters to Perú ten years ago, we taught religion in a private school for military children. But in '72 we closed the school and moved into a pueblo joven."

"WOW, what a come down!" I exclaimed in surprised admiration.

"Yes, it took a while to adjust, but we wanted to respond to CELAM's recommendation that Latin American clergy and religious sisters align themselves with the social and economic conditions of the poor. I'm happy we made the shift."

"Who or what is CELAM? I've never heard of it."

The Second Episcopal Conference of Latin American Bishops. It was held in Medellin, Columbia, in 1968, right after the Second Vatican Council and was specific to the Catholic church in Latin America," explained Sister Azalea.

"Gee, that's remarkable. Encouraging to know the Latin American bishops care about the poor."

"Yes, and as a result of CELAM, clergy and religious sisters formed Los Communidades de Base (grassroot communities) to liberate the poor from illiteracy in los pueblos jovenes."

"I've heard about these grassroot communities but didn't know our bishops were behind them."

*Lord, I thank you for bringing me to Lima and exposing me to this new information. I no longer feel alone in my desire to educate.*

Next day I walked through the crowded city and into a private clinic on a side street and asked a nurse, "Could you please direct me to the administration office?"

The nurse brought me to the female administrator who was in her fifties. "How may I help you, Sister?"

"I was wondering if you needed a nurse. I have a British RN license. I've come to Lima to obtain my Peruvian equivalency license."

She smiled. "Your guardian angel must have brought you in here. I need a night nurse. Could you work tonight?"

"Yes. I have a white uniform but I don't have white shoes."

"What size do you take?" Before I could answer she said, "Look behind my office door. I think there's a pair of white sandals that might fit you."

She was correct. They fit me fine.

"My name is Señora Alvarez," she said. "I don't have steady work for you, Sister. Each patient has her own private nurse. I'd only need you if a patient's nurse couldn't work."

"I'll be happy to fill in whenever there's a need."

Closer to Christmas I worked more shifts which earned me enough money to pay for my boarding at the convent and to finance the required nursing documents.

One evening when I wasn't working, Sister Maureen who was also staying at the Nuns' Hotel, asked, "Would you like to go for a walk?"

"Yes, I'd love to."

Sister Maureen was a couple of years younger than me but wiser and more peaceful than I was at that time. Our common bond was our deep love for the Peruvian people.

"I love the Peruvians' laid-back mañana mañana way of life," I said. "It suits me fine."

"I wanted to be missioned to Perú as soon as Pope John XXIII asked religious congregations to open a mission in South America. I didn't think they'd consider me because I hadn't made Perpetual Vows," Sister Maureen shared with sweet humility.

"Yeah, I understand. I was in a similar situation. But, we're both here now!"

"Yes. Thank God."

"I found myself when I arrived in Perú in '72. I feel Latina inside myself."

"That's how I feel as well," acknowledged Sister Maureen.

We continued walking. After we crossed a busy road Sister Maureen asked, "Kathleen, where will you do your nursing practicum for your Peruvian RN license?"

"I don't know. I know that I'm not returning to the north."

"How would you like to do your practicum where I live? I'm in a fishing city nestled in the desert hills between luscious Moquequa and Tacna. And when it rains, you'll see the desert in bloom. It's marvellous."

"Isn't Tacna on the Chilean border?" I asked. "I seem to

remember a custom's control there when I bused to Chile a few years ago."

"Yes, that's correct. Our fishing city is about 50 kilometres from the Chilean border."

"It looks like the angels are directing me from one border to another. The fishing town I came from in the north is on the Ecuador border."

"There's a government hospital a few walking blocks from our convent."

"Oh, that'd be great. Wouldn't your sisters mind me living with them for six months?"

"I've mentioned it to them and they said you'd be welcome."

"Then I accept. I'll let the registrar know I've a place for my practicum. I'll ask if I may start in February."

I arrived on a Friday, my thirty-second birthday, and commenced my practicum in the government hospital on the Monday. This fishing city was larger and more densely populated than the fishing town I left. The hospital faced the ocean. Cold waves rippled against a rocky shoreline. I missed the bounding high warm surfing waves of the northern coast with its tropical sunshine. However, the welcome I received from the sisters, the Jesuits, the Franciscans, and the locals on the three surrounding hills made up for the loss of the northern paradise.

Señora Muñoz, the head nurse in the hospital, assigned me to work with two student nurses writing their thesis, *Malnutrition: Birth to Five Years*.

Every day at 8:00 a.m. the three of us left the hospital on foot with tape measures around our necks and weighing scales under our arms. We each trudged through the streets of one hill for a week then rotated hills. Our goal was to measure and weigh as many babies and toddlers as possible. It was a daunting project, but after a week the toddlers were lined up on the dusty roads, waiting to be measured and weighed.

In the afternoons we calculated numbers and made graphs by hand. I learned that a Peruvian thesis consisted mostly of graphs with minimal writing. The resulting percentages demonstrated the level of malnutrition across the various age groups. At the end of the six months the pile of papers with graphs on both sides was divided up and bound into three soft-covered books. Because I was obtaining an equivalent license, I didn't have to defend my thesis. I had only to present it in person to the registrar at the Peruvian Nurses' Registry in Lima.

※ ※ ※

EVEN THOUGH MY PRACTICUM WAS finished, the sisters invited me to continue to live with them. I told Señora Muñoz, "I could provide prenatal care voluntarily five mornings a week in the hospital."

"Thank you, Hermana Catalina. I was hoping you'd return. You may use the room beside Dr. Sánchez's office." Dr. Sánchez was a seasoned gynaecologist who treated the poor with dignity and compassion. The women who attended my prenatal clinic were from the pueblos jovenes on the three hills.

Señora Philipa proudly shared, "We who live at the bottom of these hills are the first settlers in this pueblo joven." She continued in a contemptuous tone, "Those who live in the woven-straw houses at the top are the newcomers."

"When did the newcomers arrive?" I asked the sisters.

"Ten years ago. But settlers at the bottom of the hills still refer to them as the newcomers."

"Is the contemptuous attitude because the newcomers are from the mountains and have limited Spanish?"

"Probably," said Sister Maureen. "They don't speak Spanish well because their native tongue is Aymara or Quechua."

When these women from the high Andes attended my prenatal clinic, their husbands came as interpreters. In the Andes in the seventies, only boys went to school and learned Spanish. The hospital corridor outside my examination room became a rainbow of colours on the mornings these women had their appointments. They dressed in vibrant red, green and purple flared woollen skirts, and carried their babies in shawls wrapped around their shoulders. Their clothes complimented their ruddy complexions and high cheek bones as they leaned against the wall waiting their turn to see either Dr. Sánchez or me.

Chapter Thirty-Two

## El CLUB DE MADRES

In addition to doing a thesis during my practicum I gave weekly Charlas de Salud (health classes) to El Club de Madres in the pueblo joven.

Irrespective of which housing level on the hill a mother lived she could become a member of El Club de Madres if she paid the membership fee. On weekdays the group made two large ollas de sopa (pots of soup) for their school-aged children who would come to the hall for lunch. An individual mother couldn't afford to buy kerosene, vegetables and meat to make a nutritious soup on the money she earned from handwashing clothes or selling her wares in the marketplace. But together with all one hundred mothers contributing, El Club could provide breakfast and a nutritional soup for all their children. After my practicum I continued the weekly health classes. It gave me an opportunity to know the women and participate in their daily struggle to overcome poverty.

A woman's income for handwashing clothes ten hours a day for wealthy Peruvians or expatriates, in their homes, earned her enough money to buy a kilo of meat that day but nothing else.

*This is a photo of a typical pueblo joven of the 1970s and '80s. They were referred to as 'new developments' but essentially were impoverished areas hidden from tourists. Most had no running water other than a tap in the street or a stream nearby.*

I calculated how long a Canadian worker on minimal wage in 1978 had to work to buy a kilo of meat; only fifteen minutes. This calculation became my response for those wealthy Peruvians and expatriates who said, "The pueblo joven people are poor because they live by mañana mañana and are lazy. I've worked hard to get myself where I am. If they'd apply themselves, they could get ahead. But they choose to be squatters."

My experience of the mothers' group and the realization of this class prejudice motivated me to become a stronger advocate for those who lived in the pueblo joven. Sadly, I encountered this same prejudice in the hospital. "I fasted twelve hours yesterday but my surgery was cancelled. And I've fasted for twelve hours today but my surgery is cancelled again."

I was furious. "Señora, have you eaten anything?"

"No, Sister."

"Don't eat anything... I'll be back in a few minutes."

I consulted with Señora Muñoz before informing the hospital director. "One of your surgeons is mistreating a woman I know from El Club de Madres in the pueblo joven."

The director said, "Thank you for telling me, Sister. I've suspected this but his colleagues are reluctant to say anything negative against him."

The director himself performed the surgery on this woman that afternoon. His action was more effective than a direct reprimand of the unethical surgeon. Behind closed doors nurses and doctors thanked me for reporting this surgeon. My unique position as a religious sister and a volunteer nurse midwife in a rural government hospital with no hot water and little equipment allowed me the freedom to support not only the patients, but also my professional colleagues. I could put forward their complaints as my own and no one needed to worry about being fired. The better the rapport I had with the hospital staff, the better the pueblo joven dwellers were treated.

*The locals would use the stream, through which the cows walked, for washing their clothes, while we sisters had a cistern. The water was brought to the cistern by a truck that collected water from the stream. We placed leaves on top of the water – as the leaves sank so did the sedimentation. We called it, "the cleanest of the dirty water" and used it for clothes washing and cleaning the outhouse. The cistern is behind me in this photo as I wash clothes.*

※ ※ ※

OUR CONVENT IN THE PUEBLO joven faced a row of one-room rental suites on the roof of a neighbour's house. A young couple with their two-year-old son rented the first room. The wife was eight months pregnant when she came across the dirt road to our convent to ask, "Sister Kathleen, when my time for giving birth comes will you deliver my baby in my suite?"

"Señora, I only attend home births when there's no hospital in the area and when I've provided the prenatal care for the nine months of pregnancy. I haven't provided your prenatal care and the hospital is nearby."

Ignoring my explanation, she continued, "I had a very unpleasant experience in the hospital two years ago when I gave birth to my son. I won't go to the hospital. That's definite. If you won't deliver me, I'll find someone else or I'll deliver the baby myself."

Indignantly, she said good-bye and walked back across the road to her one-room suite. I didn't get a chance to strongly advise her not to have a home birth because there was an increased risk baby would be too big for her small pelvis. She was shorter than me, and I'm a five-footer!

A month later Marta was in advanced labour when she sent for me. I crossed the road and climbed the stairs to her room and found she was alone. "We need to go to the hospital," I told her. "I'll stay with you there."

But she refused to leave her suite. Moreover, there was no phone or any way for me to get an ambulance. Her contractions were coming fast and strong. With each contraction, she yelled, "Madre de Dios, ayudame." (Mother of God, help me.) Silently I prayed, worried the outcome wouldn't be good. She was fully dilated and pushed well but baby didn't descend.

It wasn't Mary but Sister Maureen who entered the room. I

said to her in English, "Go to the hospital and tell Señora Muñoz and the director I need an ambulance NOW."

Sister Maureen sped off to the hospital in the convent Volkswagen. Ten minutes later I heard the ambulance, but so did Marta. She gave one almighty push and now the baby's head was expelled from Marta's vagina. I was in shock. I had already removed my surgical gloves and placed my instruments in my maternity box in anticipation of transporting Marta to hospital.

The head lay in my hands but the baby's shoulders were horizontally locked in her bony pelvis. I slid my fingers into baby's right armpit trying to move the shoulder into a vertical position. I was unsuccessful. Seconds later I slid my fingers into baby's left armpit but was again unsuccessful in disengaging the shoulders. *This is a case of shoulder dystocia. I've read about this obstetrical emergency but have never seen or experienced it until now.*

"MADRE DE DIOS, AYUDAME!" Marta yelled.

I yelled even louder in English "ARE YOU BLOODY WELL DEAF?"

Sister Maureen at the head of the bed assumed I was yelling at her. She shrugged nervously. She didn't know what she was supposed to do, other than wipe Marta's forehead with a damp facecloth. With my loud yell the baby literally shot out of the pelvis and cried spontaneously. With complete relief I wrapped the baby in a towel and kept it close to me at the foot of the bed while I delivered the placenta. *I'm exhausted. I feel like **I've** given birth.*

Only when Marta asked, "Do I have a baby boy or a baby girl?" did I realize that I hadn't checked the sex nor given Marta her baby. I corrected my error – pronto!

Later while I was bathing Marta's baby boy, she asked Sister Maureen, "What did Hermana Catalina say? Whatever she said it caused my baby to be born."

Sister Maureen smirked at me and asked in English, "And how do you want me to translate what you yelled?"

Sister Maureen had figured out my yell was not directed at her but at the mother of God.

Recalling this memory at my age now makes me wonder if it wasn't the most genuine prayer I ever prayed in my life.

※ ※ ※

EVERY DAY SEEMED TO BRING new challenges. Sister Maureen came into my bedroom where I was sitting at my desk and said, "I received a cheque today from my mother for one hundred Canadian dollars. I'd like to use this money for the women in El Club de Madres. How can I do this without looking like a benefactor?"

"It's Christmas in two weeks. What about a Christmas package for each of the one hundred mothers."

"That's a good idea. What do you think the package should contain?"

"Since I'm giving health classes I think something to do with health."

"Okay."

The Canadian money was exchanged into Peruvian soles. We bought 100 bars of soap, 100 tubes of toothpaste, and 100 toothbrushes. We wrapped the packages with Peruvian-designed Christmas paper and attached a name tag to each. I wanted each mother in the group to feel special when her name was called.

After each mother received her little gift, the president of El Club de Madres, Señora Flores, thanked Sister Maureen and me on behalf of all the members. Then came the shock! "Hermana Catalina es como los perros," said Señora Flores. "Sister Kathleen is like the dogs."

I thought I must have misunderstood.

But she continued, "Because it's only the dogs who live among the poor on these dusty hills."

I share this with you because I consider this to be the greatest compliment I've ever received. It validated my feeling at home in impoverished conditions where community was our wealth.

Chapter Thirty-Three

## IN THE ANDES

Sister Maureen asked, "How would you like to bring in 1979 with my sisters and me in our mountain mission? The town is at 3,400 metres."

"You do realize 1979 is only twelve hours away, eh?"

"Yes. That's why we'd need to leave in twenty minutes," she said excitedly. "It's a four-hour drive and we need to do it while there's still daylight.

"Okay. I'll be ready at 1:00 p.m. sharp."

"Bring warm clothing as it's cold at night and in the early morning."

By 3:00 p.m. Sister Maureen and I were at the American copper mine. The government road ran through the mine. We showed our documents to the security guard who permitted us to enter the patrolled area. We drove around the rim of the mine slopes. My lips stuck together. Sister Maureen handed me a lozenge. "As we ascend to a higher altitude, we need to increase our sugar and water intake. It'll help to prevent light-headedness or a headache."

I heard what she said but was too engrossed in this new experience to comment. When I did, I said, "This is fascinating. The men in helmets down there look like midgets beside their huge yellow diggers."

"Yep, they sure do."

After we left the mine, the road was narrow, unpaved and winding.

"There's a travel restriction on these mountain roads," Sister Maureen stated. "Certain days are for going up and certain days for coming down. The road isn't wide enough to handle trucks, buses, or vehicles travelling in opposite directions."

"Today is Sunday. It's an up day, eh?"

"Yes."

We were at approximately 2,400 metres, overlooking a lake in the distance when Sister Maureen said, "OH-OH."

"What's the matter?"

"The lake is on my left and it should be on my right. We're going in the wrong direction. I have to turn around."

There was no guard rail on the cliff edge. Nothing between us and the gorge below. "You can't turn here."

"Soon it'll be dark. I've got to do it now in the daylight."

Horrified, I said, "If you're going to turn around here, I'm getting out of the car. I don't see the point of us both losing our life. One of us needs to be able to tell our families what happened."

I got out of the Volkswagen and put my back tight against the uneven rocky mountain wall. I watched without breathing as Sister Maureen did a three-point turn. When it was safe, I got back into the Volkswagen.

"We have to drive back to the mine," Sister Maureen said agitatedly. "I took the wrong road coming out."

This detour delayed us forty minutes which meant the last hour of our journey was in pitch blackness with only the car headlights to guide us. Sister Maureen hugged the mountain to stay away from the cliff edge.

We reached Cairani in the department of Tacna at 6:00 p.m. Even though Tacna is a lovely border city with Chile, the department extends high into the Andes. The Volkswagen headlights guided us over rough roads, between farms, to the convent.

When greeting us, the first thing Sister Eleanor said was, "No one drives in the Andes in the dark."

Sister Maureen smiled. "It wasn't my intention. There's a story to our arriving in the dark."

"We'll hear that later. Come on in." The convent was enclosed in a yard surrounded by a six-foot stone wall with adobe rooms around the perimeter. "This is the style of homes in the Andes," Sister Eleanor explained. "It's more economical to have adobe rooms in the yard than to have a house with rooms. The sun in the daytime heats the adobe walls. They remain warm throughout the night. Once the sun goes behind the mountain around three o'clock, kerosene lamps are used for additional heat and light."

She invited Sister Maureen and me into an adobe kitchen. It had a grey unpolished cement floor with a Tupac Amaru (revolutionary hero, and martyr of the Inca Empire) rug and a large wood stove.

Sister Tamara, the cook, said, "The lovely earthy-wood smell is from the peat moss we burn in this stove. The locals get the peat moss from la pampa." (The grassy wetlands in the Andes.)

"It smells nice," I said.

"The locals also maintain the alfafa and potato farms for the wealthy farm owners who underpay them," commented Sister Eleanor.

"That's horrible," I said before asking, "Where is the bathroom?"

"The abode room to your left."

"Thank you."

When I closed the kitchen door behind me, I looked up,

exhilarated by the immense star-filled sky. *There're more stars than sky. I can almost touch them they're so low. OH WOW, there's the Southern Cross and the Milky Way.*

"Tomorrow you'll need to put on long-johns, a layer of sweaters, under an alpaca poncho before the sun disappears. Do you have warm clothing, Sister Kathleen?" asked Sister Eleanor.

"Yes, but not a poncho."

"We can borrow Sister Agnes's poncho for you. She's on home leave in Canada. The trick is to put on extra clothes before you feel chilly. If you wait until you feel chilly you won't warm up for the rest of the evening."

"Thanks, Sister Eleanor. I'll be sure to dress warmly tomorrow afternoon before the sun sets."

Sister Eleanor grinned. "In the high altitude there's no sunrise or sunset. The sun appears and disappears rapidly."

Sister Tamara added, "In the morning we stay in our arctic sleeping bags until the sun appears over the mountain. Then we get up."

Not being a morning person, I said, "That sounds good to me."

Except I didn't get to sleep in. At 5:00 a.m. Sister Maureen banged on my bedroom door. "Kathleen, wake up. Hurry and get dressed," she said loudly. "La doctora from the government clinic is here. She's asking for us to drive a woman in labour down the mountain."

*This lady doctor is probably an intern doing her practicum. I bet that she has little or no maternity experience.*

Sister Maureen continued, "The baby's foot is outside the vagina. Hurry, Kathleen. We'll use the sisters' jeep."

Opening the bedroom door while pulling the sleeve of my jacket over my backward extended arm, I told Sister Maureen, "We AREN'T driving this woman down the mountain."

"We have to... the doctora has no vehicle."

*Sister Killian told me contractions accelerate for a labouring mother in a vehicle. That's what happened to poor Philomena! So we aren't taking this woman anywhere... especially not in a jeep.*

Dr. Santos, along with her thick-framed auxiliary nurse, Beatrix, and I waited anxiously in the cold early hours of the morning for Sister Maureen to back the jeep out of the makeshift carport.

"We're delivering the woman in her house." I told Dr. Santos. "It's too dangerous to move her."

"We'll see when we get there," Dr. Santos said and climbed hastily into the front passenger seat. I squeezed into the rear seat with Beatrix and we set off.

A few minutes later Dr. Santos shouted to Sister Maureen, "STOP, here's the house."

The abrupt skid on the gravel sent a cloud of dust into the crisp morning air. An elderly farmer dressed in a poncho and sombrero was smoking his pipe at the entrance of the house. Dr. Santos, Beatrix, and I rushed toward the front door. Dr. Santos pushed it open... only to find a yard full of chickens. She pushed open three more doors surrounding the yard before realizing we were in the wrong house! In exasperation the doctora waved her arms over her head and brought them down in a swift semi-circular movement, a classical Peruvian gesture of annoyance.

Sister Maureen didn't use this annoyance gesture but calmly explained to the elderly man, "La doctora is in a hurry to help a woman in childbirth. In our anxiety we came to the wrong house. Sorry."

He tipped his sombrero in acknowledgement and we drove on. Within a few moments we were at the correct house.

"Would you attend this birth, Sister Kathleen?" Dr. Santos asked. "If anything goes wrong the people won't turn on the sisters. If I do the delivery and something goes wrong, they'll turn on me."

"Yes, I'll attend this birth. I understand."

To my great relief no foot was externally visible. But 10 toes were at the door, and the umbilical cord wrapped around the ankles. Gulp! I looked at the husband. "Could you ask your wife to lie across the bed? Her buttocks have to be at the edge. And could you support her back with your thighs?"

I grabbed a flannel shirt from the nearby pile of clothes on the chair, thinking of Dr. Bhatt in England. *I'll use this shirt to trick baby into thinking it's still in the womb the way he taught me to do when delivering a breech.*

Fortunately, this Aymara woman's birth canal was spacious. It was her third pregnancy. She gave two or three pushes and baby was born up to the neck. Baby hung from the womb inside the shirt. I could feel movement and held the umbilical cord close. With the final contraction and a gentle push from the mother I slowly delivered the head. I motioned to the father to remove the shirt. When he did, he exclaimed in Aymara, "We have a girl."

They were thrilled as they had two boys. I nicknamed this baby girl, Corona, because the umbilical cord was in a circle on top of her head as well as around her ankles.

Sister Maureen invited Dr. Santos and Beatrix to the convent for breakfast. We retold the tale to Sisters Eleanor and Tamara of how we went into the wrong house in our state of panic.

Chapter Thirty-Four

## WALKING THE STREETS

In the nineteen-eighties, temporary professed sisters spent three months in a mission country before pronouncing their perpetual vows. Sisters Sonia and Pauline had come to Perú from the Netherlands. Sister Sonia accompanied me on home visits. We walked side by side on the loose dirt road in the pueblo joven.

Then without warning she stopped. "Ooohhh... I sow a vary ugly child."

"Ugly?"

She touched her own top lip. "A hole!"

*Oh, dear Jesus. The child must have a hare lip and cleft palate.*

"Where was the child?" I asked.

Sister Sonia stood transfixed and pointed to an estera (straw) house with a crude wood door. The wire hinges were old and the door hung at an angle. "She's gone."

"How old was this child?"

"Mawbe two."

"Did she go into this house?"

"I dawen't know."

I walked towards the sloped door and thumped it with my

palm. A woman dressed in a wide woollen skirt with a shawl around her shoulders and a bowler hat atop her long black braids opened the door and stared at me in silence.

"Señora, you know we're sisters and I'm a nurse in the hospital. I'm looking for a small child with an open space between her nose and mouth. Do you have such a child in your home?"

I knew that any child with a deformity would be hidden from the public.

She said, "No."

"Have you seen such a child in any other house around here?"

"No."

*She sure isn't going to tell me. But I'm just as determined to find this child as she is to hide what she knows.*

I tore a piece of paper from a pocket notebook and wrote my name and address on it. I handed her the jagged piece of paper. "Por se acaso (Just in case) you happen to see this child, please come to our convent and ask for me."

Sister Sonia and I continued walking. I needed to get to Nati's house before lunch. I was on the last day of administering eardrops to her little girl's infected ear.

At Nati's house I examined Miranda's ear and said, "Nati, if this infection returns, please let me know."

This is precisely what happened. The little girl's ear started oozing a week after treatment. I took her to see Dr. Gomez, the ears, nose and throat specialist.

Dr. Gomez looked inside the infected ear. "Hermana Catalina, did you have a chest x-ray done on Miranda?"

Alarmed by his question that suggested he saw tuberculosis in Miranda's ear, I said, "No I didn't."

"Then please have one done."

Nati and I brought Miranda to the hospital. The chest x-ray

was positive for tuberculosis. Now I knew why the antibiotic eardrops hadn't cured Miranda's infected ear.

Nati and I held each other in sorrow. I stooped to Miranda's height, "Miranda, if you're a big girl and don't cry when Mommy and I leave you here in the hospital, I'll bring you a doll to sleep with tonight."

Her eyes danced with delight. She didn't have a doll, but she longed to have one. Miranda's lower lip quivered as her mother and I left her bedside.

"Do you know where I could get a doll?" I asked Sister Maureen. "I promised Miranda I'd bring her a doll tonight."

"The American children must have dolls they no longer play with," she said. "They will probably give us one for Miranda." Sister Maureen taught Catechism to American children in the American smelter gated community.

"You're right. Let's try there."

Inside the gates parents were dressing their children in Halloween costumes.

"They really do live in another world," I whispered to Sister Maureen. "They aren't going to appreciate our request for a doll in the midst of their celebrations."

Sister Maureen shrugged her shoulders as we approached the screen door of one of the luxurious company houses. "I know the American woman who lives here," she said and pressed the doorbell.

The Peruvian housekeeper ushered us into a sitting room and announced, "Señora Tammy, there are two sisters here to see you."

Tammy was a tall slender lady. She came in with a little girl of about eight who was wearing a Bambi costume. She introduced herself to me and said, "This is my daughter, Sylvanna. Because we're from Pennsylvania." She smiled. "My husband, Don, is an engineer with the mining company."

I said, "Pleased to meet you, Tammy, and you too, Sylvanna. I'm Sister Kathleen and I live in community with Sister Maureen."

"Sorry, Tammy, for the intrusion," Sister Maureen said, "but we need your help."

Tammy and her daughter listened as I explained the situation.

"Sister, you can give Miranda my Cabbage Patch doll," Sylvanna said. "Hope she gets better soon." Then she hopped like a deer out of the room.

The doll was dressed in pink overalls, with a pink-and-green plaid shirt, and sported brown pigtails. It was perfect.

In the hospital, Miranda hugged her doll and kept it in her arms for the remainder of her stay. The tuberculosis medication was effective but couldn't restore her hearing loss. She remained permanently deaf in her left ear. But that didn't stop her from playing with other children on her street or later from attending school.

※ ※ ※

As for the mysterious child with the hare lip and cleft palate, two weeks later an Aymara couple came to the convent and asked for me. When I entered the sitting room, the woman handed me the torn piece of paper. "I'm Naira. This is my husband, Freddie. The little girl with the bad face is our daughter."

Freddie said, "My wife said you want to help us."

I hugged both of them as was customary.

"Yes. The Saint John of God Hospital in Arequipa does free surgery for children from pueblos jovenes. What's your little girl's name? How old is she?"

"Jasmina. She is two years and eight months."

"Your little girl needs surgery as soon as possible. Normally, this kind of surgery is done in the first year of life."

"We didn't know surgery could fix this," Naira said. "We

thought an evil spirit did this to her because we didn't put a red string on her wrist when she was born."

"No. This happened in the first few months of pregnancy when baby was being formed. They don't know the cause. But it's more common than you think. Jasmina will meet other children with this condition in the hospital."

Freddie and Naira held each other's gaze. Freddie asked, "How much does the bus cost? Where will Naira and Jasmina stay?"

I explained, "We as missionary sisters receive donation money from people in different countries to pay for situations like this. I'll ask to use some donation money to buy bus tickets, medicines, and lodgings in a hostel near the hospital. I'll go with you, Naira."

The bus ride was a new experience for Jasmina. She pointed at cows, horses and sheep dogs but didn't speak.

When we got to the hospital, Naira assured the paediatric surgeon, "Jasmina can speak but she doesn't pronounce words clearly either in Aymara or Spanish.

"After surgery, Jasmina will require speech therapy," the surgeon informed her. "It will be easier if you speak only Spanish with her. When she starts school, the official language will be Spanish. Later in life she can learn Aymara."

Naira nodded.

The surgery was done in stages over the next year and a half. Jasmina had a permanent scar between her nose and top lip, but she was able to pronounce words clearly and eat normally.

※ ※ ※

WALKING THE STREETS BROUGHT ME in contact with yet another child who needed to be accompanied to Saint John of God Hospital. This time it was Fiona, an amazing youngster who walked on her hands with an arched back and protruding bum. I smiled. *I remember playing like this when I was a kid.*

But when Fiona sat down her legs crumpled like a puppet's legs, I realized she wasn't playing. *Oh my God, this youngster has polio.*

"Hola," I said.

"Hola, Señora." She had tantalizing green eyes under a Shirley Temple head of tight black curls.

"Do you live in this house?"

"Yes. I live here with my mother, my older brother, and sister."

"Is your mother home?"

"No, she's at work. But my sister is here. Do you want to talk to her?" Before I could answer she hollered, "Pamela, una señora wants to talk to you."

"Pamela," I said, "could you ask your mother to come to the convent tomorrow, please? I'd like to talk with her."

"Yes, I'll tell her, Sister."

The next afternoon Estella came to the convent. She said Fiona had walked on her hands for the last eight years of her life, causing her legs to become two strong pillars.

"Fiona may be able to walk upright with braces," I explained. "The braces won't cost you anything. We need to take Fiona to Saint John of God Hospital."

Estella's eyes filled with tears of joy. "She will walk?"

The orthopaedic surgeon examined Fiona and said, "Amazing. This girl has strengthened her legs by walking on her hands. I'm pleased she wasn't in a wheelchair or carried."

"Will braces help my Fiona?" Estella asked.

"Indeed they will. We'll measure her for braces today. The braces will have to change as she continues to grow." Then to Fiona he said, "You're a trooper. You'll do well in life."

And she did.

*This darling child (referred to as Fiona in this memoir) has polio from the waist down. I saw her 'walking' on her hands dragging her legs behind her.*

## Chapter Thirty-Five

## DISTRAUGHT

"You'll be fine, Fatima. I'm sorry that I'll miss your delivery but I'll come visit you and your new baby as soon as I return."

Every year we sisters went for our annual retreat to the beautiful city of Miraflores (look at the flowers). I looked forward to ten days of community with the sisters and the spiritual renewal in Liberation Theology. This is a theology focused on the liberation of the poor from social injustices and human rights violations. Even though it was frowned on by both the official Catholic church in Latin America and by the papacy, at that time, because of its roots in Marxism, the conference centre was crowded for the talks by Father Gustavo Gutierrez OP with priests, sisters and laity from los pueblos jovenes. In later chapters you will read how a dedication to live amongst the poor brought about the death of priests, sisters and laity in Latin American countries.

Fatima had never missed a prenatal appointment in her nine months. On every visit she'd ask, "Hermana Catalina, you'll deliver me, won't you?"

I'd humour her and say "Yes. Of course."

*Who's she kidding? Her husband is a corporate manager in the American mines. He'll want his wife, Tima, (pronounced Tee ma) as he was fond of calling her, to deliver in the modern well-equipped hospital for employees of the American mining company. He won't allow her to deliver in our poor ill-equipped government hospital with no hot water or neonatal intensive care unit.*

I was wrong. They chose the government hospital.

Tima was in early labour on the morning of the day I returned from Miraflores. In the evening I walked up the sloped corridor to the postnatal unit. A postnatal nurse greeted me. "Hermana Cati, who are you here to visit?"

"Fatima."

"Fatima hasn't had her baby yet. She's in the pre-op room. She's to be sectioned soon."

"WHAT? I exclaimed. "Who is doing the C-section?"

"Dr. Ramirez."

*This is good. He and I work very well together. He's my favourite physician in this hospital. I'll be able to talk to him and buy Tima some time and hopefully avoid a C-section.*

When I opened the door to the narrow pre-op room, Tima was having a contraction. She yelled loudly as she rolled from side to side. From the foot of the bed, I said in an authoritative voice, "FATIMA, calm down."

"Hermana Catalina," Tima said in a whiney voice.

Dr. Ramirez and I met in the corridor outside the pre-op room.

"How come she hasn't an IV? She needs to be hydrated. How's the fetal heart? What's the dilation?"

"Hermana Catalina, slow down. I've just taken over this case with the shift change. I'll start an IV now. I'm told she's 5 centimetres dilated since 1:00 p.m. today. It's now 6:00 p.m. The fetal heart has remained regular."

"Dr. Ramirez, the failure of dilation is completely

psychological. Fatima has gotten herself into a negative emotional state. For nine months she has had her heart set on me delivering her baby. Could you give me two hours to work with her? If she isn't fully dilated by then, she can be C-sectioned. Would you agree to this?"

"Yes, I'll give you two hours but not a minute more."

I laughed. "You sound like Portia telling Shylock in *The Merchant of Venice*, 'You may have a pound of flesh but not a drop of blood.' Thanks, Dr. Ramirez."

In the pre-op room, Tima was very happy to see me return. She was hydrated and had energy due to the increased amount of glucose in her body.

"Take slow deep breaths at the start of a contraction and throughout its duration," I said. "I'll keep my hand over your uterus and tell you when to start the slow deep breaths."

"Okay, I can do this."

We worked as a team for the next two hours.

At 8 o'clock I asked, "Tima, may I examine you?"

"Yes."

The cervix was fully dilated. Baby was happy. Tima was transferred to the delivery room. Dr. Ramirez stood by my side and Frank, a tall well-built Texan, stood by Tima's side holding her hand. Forty-five minutes later she gave birth to a healthy baby girl.

Dr. Ramirez sutured the episiotomy. "It's quicker to suture this incision than a C-section incision," he joked.

This was true. I nicknamed their baby girl, Miraflores, since she had waited for my return from that city to come into the world.

※ ※ ※

As emotionally attached to the hospital staff as I was after working with them every day for five years, I was aware of the atmosphere deteriorating. The director, who had treated the poor with respect and dignity, had retired and the new director had an authoritarian style of leadership. In other words, he was a dictator. The hospital atmosphere was no longer relaxed.

Patients sensed the tension. One day an Aymara prenatal patient (who lived in a different pueblo joven to where I lived) told me, "An elderly woman who isn't known to us appears to be dying on a slab of wood on the dirt road. I think she needs help."

"Have you told the hospital social worker?" I asked.

"No. I'm telling you because I know you come to our pueblo joven often. The social worker never comes."

"I'll ask the new director if I may use an ambulance to bring the woman here. Thanks for telling me."

I knocked on the director's office door.

"Adelante."

He sat in a high-back leather chair behind a large mahogany desk.

After cordially greeting him, I asked, "May I please have the use of an ambulance to bring a dying woman to the emergency room?"

The director raised his top lip at the right and lowered his bottom lip at the left in a kind of lopsided smile to demonstrate he was in control of this situation. "Hermana, I can't spare an ambulance for a dying woman," he said slowly. "Ambulances are to assist the living."

"Oh, I see. You prefer that this woman dies like a dog on the road than dirty the name of the hospital with a death."

He wheeled his chair back. "If you please, you don't need to speak like that."

"It's fine," I said. "I appreciate knowing your stance on the use of ambulances." I turned and left his office.

On the main street, three blocks from the hospital, I hailed a taxi. "I don't have any money in my uniform pocket. But you know I'm a sister and we can go to the convent later for the fare. Right now, I need to be taken up to the top of the sandy hills. I need to bring a dying woman into hospital."

"I don't like to drive on those sandy slopes," the taxi driver said. "It's not good for my car. My car is my livelihood." He paused, considering. "But for you, Sister, I'll do it. I know you help my people."

We drove slowly up and up and up until we reached the top. There we saw the wrinkled skinny woman with matted hair on a slab of wood, by the side of the road. She was unconscious. The taxi driver pulled over. "Sister, seat yourself in the back and leave the door open."

I did as he said. I watched him gently put his right arm under the woman's neck and his left arm under her knees to carry her to the taxi and lower her thin body onto my lap. Her head naturally fell onto my shoulder. In silence we drove down the hill to the hospital. Dr. Ramirez appeared at the hospital entrance with an orderly and a gurney. We wheeled the woman into a small room in the emergency department.

Once the door was closed, he said, "Hermana Catalina, one day that director will need a doctor but none of us will lift a finger to help him." He admitted the woman to the female medical unit.

I took the taxi to the convent, and the driver and I had tea together before he left with a generous payment. *This man is the good shepherd for me today.*

The next morning, the woman hadn't been bathed or changed into a hospital gown. I asked an auxiliary nurse why and she told me, "Sister, you didn't bring in any soap, towel or clothes."

"Do families have to supply everything when a loved one is admitted to hospital?"

"Sí. Including eating utensils."

We used half a pillowcase and a sliver of carbolic soap to wash the woman and used the other half to dry her. I went to the convent to fetch a new pair of flowered cotton pajamas I'd received in the mail from my mother earlier in the week. I returned to the female medical unit and dressed the woman in the pajamas. She looked lovely even though she was still unconscious.

She never regained consciousness. The hospital chaplain gave her the Sacrament of the Sick and she died that evening with dignity.

Chapter Thirty-Six

## INSPIRATIONAL TEENAGERS

The Catholic Youth Group consisted of young men and women between fourteen and twenty years of age. The women outnumbered the men three to one. But the men were as committed as the women to teaching catechism to the children in the three pueblos jovenes. Suzanna was one of the leaders. I often heard her remind new members, "Don't worry about getting everything perfect. Make the time you spend with the children playful and loving." It wasn't surprising the group elected her to represent them at the Catholic Youth Conference in Lima in the summer of '82.

Sister Maureen also attended the conference. When they returned, Sister Maureen told me, "I think Suzanna is not well. At night I heard her coughing in the dormitory. One night I went to see if I could help and found her sweating profusely. Yet she didn't have a high fever. What do you think it could be, Kathleen?"

"It sounds like tuberculosis. I'll take her to the hospital in the morning for a chest x-ray." Because I was a Peruvian RN, I could order bloods or x-rays without first consulting with a physician.

The next day, the respiratory physician read the x-ray and confirmed Suzanna had TB.

"Are you going to admit her?"

"I can't admit everyone to hospital with the first signs of TB. Eighty percent of this fishing city has TB. I have to keep beds for the most critical. She can recuperate at home with medication and bedrest."

Sister Maureen drove Suzanna and me to her house and I explained to her mother that her daughter was to be on complete bedrest.

Later that same night Suzanna's brother came to the convent in a state of hysteria. He cried, "Suzanna's dying. She vomited blood."

Sister Maureen and I were beside ourselves with worry as we drove to Suzanna's house.

"Help her into the Volkswagen," I said. "We've got to get her to the hospital as quickly as possible."

I carried the potty with the blood carefully to the Volkswagen. In the emergency department I showed the potty to the emergency physician. I asked, "Will you please admit Suzanna? Earlier today her chest x-ray showed positive for tuberculosis."

"Yes. Bring her in."

Suzanna remained in hospital for three months. When she was ambulatory, she met another youth in the hospital who also had TB. I visited her often.

"Hermana, I met Vicente who plays the guitar and sings. I asked him to join our youth group when we get better. He said he'd like that."

"Yes, I know Vicente. He has a lovely voice. He'd be a great addition to the youth group."

Vicente was sixteen when I first heard him sing in the park bandstand. Teenage girls swooned at the foot of the stage, but Vicente seemed unaware of how his voice and good looks affected these girls. He was too shy to make eye contact with them or be flirtatious. Mostly he looked down at his guitar. When he finished singing, he slowly and laboriously walked away.

Six months later Vicente was hospitalized with TB of the hip.

Dr. Fernando said to me, "Hermana Catalina, this teenager needs a nutritious diet, a battery of medications, and eventually will need a total hip replacement."

"Vicente is from one of the poorest families in the pueblo joven," I shared. "He's the oldest of three siblings. His father is often away as a fisherman. His mother counts on the money Vicente gets from singing. I'll talk with the sisters and see what we can do to help him get nutritious food and medicines."

"Gracias, Hermana."

I walked heavy-heartedly to the four-bed male unit.

Vicente was sitting on his bed strumming his guitar. He smiled enthusiastically. "Hola, Hermana Catalina, I've composed a new song. Let me play it for you."

His face shone with inner strength and joy.

*Jesus, have mercy on me for losing my joy in the face of so much suffering. Thank you for bringing Vicente into my life to remind me to sing through the pain.*

At our sisters' community meeting I said, "Dr. Fernando has asked if we could help Vicente with food and medicines."

"Does he have TB in the lungs as well as the hip?" Sister Maureen asked.

"No, surprisingly the chest x-ray showed his lungs are clear."

A sister suggested, "If Vicente would like to stay in our convent in the Andes when he's discharged from the hospital, I'm sure we could arrange this for him. The air will be healthier in the mountains than here in our fishing city where the pollution from the smelter is bad. Our city had the highest number of TB cases per capita in the country."

One of the sisters pointed out. "In the Andean convent, Vicente

*A wonderful teenager (referred to as Vicente in this story) continued to sing joyfully as TB consumed him.*

would be able to sit outdoors in the sunshine and have his own room which he probably wouldn't have at home."

Sister Brenda, the bursar, said, "Our donation funds will pay for nutritious food and medicines whether he stays here at home or in our Andean convent."

Vicente chose to convalesce in the mountains. But after seven months of convalescence, we heard from Sister Tamara that even though Vicente was eating three nutritious meals a day and high protein milk shakes twice a day, he had failed to gain weight.

"I've contacted the Mayo Clinic in Rochester, Minnesota, regarding a total hip replacement for Vicente after his convalescence. They have agreed to do the surgery *pro bono*." I told Sister Tamara.

"Oh, this is wonderful news, Sister Kathleen. Maybe he'll start to gain weight with this new incentive."

"I sure hope so. He'll have to have a recent chest x-ray before travelling."

Sadly this second chest x-ray showed positive for TB. This was devastating news for Vicente, his family, and us sisters. Vicente decided to return home and spend his remaining months with his family.

After Vicente's burial I told Sister Tamara, "The grief I experienced when Vicente died was similar to the grief I experienced in 1959 when Richie Valens was killed in the plane crash with Buddy Holly and the Big Bopper. Vicente, like Richie Valens, was seventeen years old, Latino, good looking, a music composer, and a singer."

Now, whenever I hear Richie Valens' songs, I think of Vicente and hope that both of them are singing together in Heaven.

※ ※ ※

Donation money was used mostly for buying anti-tuberculosis medicines. We had to prioritize patients for whom we'd buy the medicines. These were painful decisions to make. We decided mothers and youth were priority. *If we lose a mother, there are more orphaned children. Youth are Perú's future.*

Rosario was fourteen years old when Helena, her mother, was hospitalized and she had to take care of her five younger siblings. The youngest was 11 months old. The two-year-old cried incessantly.

"Tito, Mummy is in hospital," Rosario would tell him. "She needs to get better."

*'Helena' with her children. She recorded her voice before she died of TB so that her youngest children could know their mother's voice. On the right is Sister Sonia (RIP) who accompanied me on many home visits.*

"But why can't she come home."

"Remember when you had a boo-boo on your knee? You went to the hospital and came home all better. When Mummy is all better, she'll come home just like you did."

This explanation satisfied him for a little while. Then the crying and sometimes screaming would start again.

Helena had advanced tuberculosis in both lungs. She sat forward in the bed to breathe easier. There were no pillows to support her bony frame. She had sunken eyes.

I sat on the end of her bed. "What can I do for you, Helena?"

"Help Rosario. Tell her I'm sorry she's had to drop out of school to take care of her brothers and sisters."

"I can do that, Helena. I think she already knows you wish you could change this situation. Perhaps, if I go to the market for her. It'll be one less chore for her to do."

Helena gave a weak smile and nodded. She didn't have the air to speak. She needed to rest.

"I'll come back tomorrow." I prayed an Our Father, a Hail Mary and a Glory Be to the Father while holding her hands before I left her.

I returned the next day with a tape recorder. "Helena, let me show you how to record your voice. It's easy. Press this button to record and the stop button when you finish."

"I've never heard my voice. What will it sound like?"

"Let's see." She giggled on hearing her voice.

"You can record a sentence at a time whenever you feel up to it," I said. "Your children need to hear your voice when you're not with them. It'll comfort them and assure them how much you love them."

Helena reached for my hands. She squeezed them as a thank-you. She completed one side of the tape for her children in the weeks before she died.

# PART V

## SCOTLAND TO THE ALTIPLANO

## Chapter Thirty-Seven

## REQUALIFICATION

In August of 1983, after four years in Perú a visit home was on the horizon. The weather was cool when I took the 24-hour bus ride to Lima and stayed overnight in the Nuns' Hotel before taking the plane the next day to Canada.

Although it was very hot and humid when I arrived in Montreal, it was wonderful to stay at my mother's apartment and visit with the extended family. In my absence babies had been born into the clan. A joy to come to know them.

Before I could return to Perú, the leadership team, as it was called after Vatican II, suggested I take a refresher course in midwifery. Since Canada at that time didn't have such a program I chose to go to Scotland.

*I haven't communicated with Drew for seven years. I can't be in England and not be reunited with him, so I'll avoid the temptation. I need to let our affection for each other remain in the past.*

I lived in the Perth nurses' residence and went by train to our convent in Glasgow on my days off. The sisters received me graciously into their community. I loved the Scottish accent even though at times I couldn't make out what people were saying, especially on the train when passengers spoke in broad Scots.

Staff Nurse McPherson said, "Nurse Kelly, Mrs. Pollock and her bairn need your help. Could you please attend to them?"

"Yes, Nurse McPherson."

I realized the bairn was the baby.

"Nurse Kelly, you'll find the bairn's goonie in the chest of drawers next to the crib."

I assumed a 'goonie' was the baby's gown.

The midwifery program I had taken ten years earlier had been replaced by a two-year program. I was permitted to do one year of the two-year program. *Oh Lord, how did the natural process of childbirth become so technical? Help me, Jesus, to cope. I feel lost in this strange world of technology.*

Disillusioned with my profession, I phoned Father Drew's parish house. I was prepared to speak with the housekeeper and politely ask to speak with Father Drew. Instead, when the phone stopped ringing, I heard "St. Bonaventure Parish. Father Drew speaking."

My heart raced. All my intentions abandoned me. I tried to control my breathing. "Hello."

I didn't get to say another word. I heard a loving laugh. "Is that you, Katie?" he asked excitedly.

"Yes."

"Where are you?"

"In Scotland."

"When can I see you?"

Still nervous about seeing him I said, "A lot has happened in seven years, Drew."

"Of course. A lot has happened for me too in seven years. When can I see you?"

I caved and agreed to take the train to England on my next days off.

Drew was at the station when the train pulled in. It was thrilling to be able to look at him before he'd seen me. As soon as I was on the platform, we hugged and he said, "Oh, Katie, it's wonderful to see you. You're thinner but still beautiful, my love. Hope you're not too cold. It's rained here all day. Let me get you to the presbytery. I had the housekeeper make us supper."

We walked to the car under his large black umbrella. He held the car door open for me. When the car was in motion and Drew was concentrating on the wet roads with the wipers swishing, I glanced sideways at him. I'll never forget the adrenaline surge I felt. *Your head can tell you one thing, but your heart tells a different story.* For the first time I knew how deeply I loved Drew. Up until this moment I'd been in love with being loved. I had loved the attention and affection Drew showered on me. But in that moment, I experienced the depth of my love for this man… this priestly man.

After supper we sat quietly in each other's arms.

"Did Sister Hyacinth tell you not to correspond with me?" Drew asked.

"Yes."

"I thought so. Because it was shortly after she went to Perú that you asked me to no longer write to you. I respected your request but had the feeling it didn't come from you."

In silence I gazed at him with such intensity that his facial features engraved themselves in my memory; they will be there forever.

"It's okay, Katie. You did what you thought at the time was what you were supposed to do. I love you whether I hear from you or not. My affection for you will never change."

Then he laughed and brought me closer. My head rested on his chest. "Distance makes the heart grow fonder."

*Yep, I guess that's what's happened to my heart.*

On my return to Scotland I felt optimistic and even grateful for the demanding refresher course because it had brought Drew and me together again. The course wasn't the enemy. *I'll embrace technology as my helper not as my replacement.*

With this shift in thinking my fear of the big white machine beside my patient's bed with graft paper hanging from its mouth, left me. I learned to read the thin-lined drawings on the paper. *It's fascinating how the arm draws a perfect V-shape telling me baby's heartbeat is strong during mother's contractions.*

But at 23:00 hours one night the arm didn't draw a perfect V during a contraction. The needle hesitated at the bottom of the V. *Oh Mother of God, this is what they call a TYPE 1 dip. Now I get it. Baby is telling me it's having a hard time getting oxygen during the contraction.* I left the room and went to the central nursing station.

"Excuse me, Sister, could you please come and check the fetal monitor. I think there's a TYPE 1 dip."

She confirmed this diagnosis and paged the obstetrician. He was in the room ten minutes later performing a forceps lift-out delivery. The pediatrician administered oxygen to the baby via a face mask. After a few breaths baby cried well. That night I appreciated how technology had saved the life of this baby.

※ ※ ※

MY LAST VISIT WITH DREW was heart-breaking. I left Glasgow on the early morning train for Manchester. As we drove to the presbytery I was already grieving as I suspected it'd be our last time together. We spent the nights in separate rooms but in the mornings, before he celebrated the 8:00 a.m. mass, we cuddled in his bed.

On the last morning, Drew said, "Katie, don't be sad. I'm right here beside you. Remember what Jesus told the apostles. 'It isn't the time to grieve when the bridegroom is with you. There'll be time later when He's gone to grieve.' Let's enjoy and celebrate this moment together."

I wasn't as brave. The tears rolled down my face onto the pillow. We kissed slowly and tenderly. It was indeed the last time we were ever together.

Chapter Thirty-Eight

# A JESUIT TEAM

Fr. Juan Luis, director of the Jesuit International Educational Team in our fishing city, came to the convent as he knew that I had just returned from Scotland and wanted to offer me a new position before the sisters suggested that I return to the hospital and El Club de Madres.

"Catalina, as you know our team consists of twenty-six women and men, mostly Peruvians. Our night classes are in soldering for male labourers, also journalism and photography, and adult academic education, in addition to our pastoral work. Our focus is on social justice and human rights. The population we work with are the poor in the three pueblos jovenes."

"Yes, I'm aware of the team's commitment to the poor and to social justice issues," I commented.

"I invite you to join our team. We need an educator in health issues. Are you interested?"

"Yes! I'd consider it an honour to be a member of the team. But my Spanish is limited."

"Don't worry about that. You may not use grammatically correct Spanish but your passion to fight for human dignity speaks loud and clear even in broken Spanish." He raised his eyebrows. That made me laugh. It was a typical Juan Luis facial expression.

"We challenge the status quo, the church and the government when we see any blatant injustice to the poor. We don't participate in demonstrations but support demonstrators if their protest is for a just cause."

"I remember the workers' hunger strike," I said. "Some of the workers were hospitalized when I worked there."

"Yes, that was a terrible time. Thank you for supporting the workers. I heard about your involvement. You're a registered Peruvian nurse and a midwife. Is this correct?"

"I'm a Peruvian nurse but not a Peruvian midwife," I acknowledged. "My midwifery license is from Scotland."

"You'll be an asset to the women's section on our team. Some women you'll work with will be challenging. Two of them were political prisoners before becoming members of our team. But they're also fun-loving and well respected in El Club de Madres and the community as a whole. I have my motorcycle outside. Can you come now to the centre with me so that I can introduce you to your companeros de trabajo?"

"Okay."

"Hop on the back."

He waited for me to put a helmet on and seat myself behind him before starting the motorcycle. I had seen team members going to their night classes on motorcycles. It seemed the most practical mode of transportation at night in the pueblos jovenes.

When we got to the centre Juan Luis said, "We gather daily here for a snack between 6:00 and 6:30, before night classes at 7:00. It's our comrade time."

Inside, members stood around the table eating bread buns dipped in fresh mashed avocado. I knew several by sight but not by name. Juan Luis introduced me to them one by one.

*The Jesuit International Educational Team of which I was a member for four years. Far right, top row is the director, Fr. Juan Luis SJ, (Argentinian). I am in the middle row, third from left. Fr. Santiago (Peruvian) is the smiling man with sunglasses to my right. Our focus was on human rights and social justice in the pueblos jovenes. Some members had been political prisoners because terrorist groups, the government, the Catholic church at that time and the military all saw us as subversives.*

Each in turn said, "Welcome, Cati."

Some of the guys were obviously teasers and free-spirited. They created a relaxed atmosphere in the small lunchroom. After their break everyone hurried to get wherever they were supposed to be for 7:00 p.m.

Petra, leader of the women's section, said, "Cati, come sit here and chat. I don't have a class until 8:00. Would you like a mate, and a bun with avocado?"

"I'd love a cup of mate."

Petra and I talked about the work format and goals of the women's section.

"Our goal is to liberate mothers in the pueblos jovenes through education."

"I agree," I said. "Education is the door to freedom."

She continued, "Classes are from 7:00 p.m. to 10:00 p.m. three nights a week. Tonight is the first sewing class. In the first hour we teach the mothers to make a pattern template for a school uniform. In the second hour, the mothers will learn to sew the uniform. We provide the treadle sewing machines, and thread. The mothers buy the material. In the third hour a speaker does a presentation on a current social justice or human rights issue. I anticipate you could present health issues in this time slot. Have you any ideas of health issues pertaining to women's rights?"

I didn't have to think long. "I'm not prepared to talk tonight, but yes, I have several."

"Great. Can you start next week?"

"Yes."

"Let's discuss your ideas at our weekly Thursday morning meeting. It runs from 9:00 until noon."

On Thursday, seven of us women seated ourselves around a circular table in the corner of a room off a long, wide, well-lit corridor of classrooms.

Petra commenced the meeting by saying, "Please introduce yourselves to Cati. We know she's a sister, but just like Juan Luis her title is dropped." She looked at me. "Juan Luis strongly believes in equality among members. So even though he is director he has asked that we do not call him padre."

Each woman introduced herself to me and shared how long she had been a member of the team and what her role was in the group. When the introductions finished each member reported what her week had been like since the previous Thursday meeting. After each sharing, the listening six members voiced their opinions on what was shared.

"Not all the women had material to sew," Lucia said. "My solution was to have two women work together at a sewing machine. This made it less noticeable who had material and who didn't."

"I think you handled an awkward situation tactfully."

"Yeah, I agree."

"Did you ask the women privately when they'd have the material?"

"Should we make sure a woman can afford the material before enrollment for future courses?"

This question opened another discussion.

"Let's move on," said Petra. "Los clubes de madres and women's groups from Lima have contacted me. The government has put up billboards featuring a rabbit in the centre and an Andean woman in the top corner with Family Planning in bold letters at the bottom.

"The government is reducing us to rabbits?"

"That's disgusting."

"Apparently this billboard is in every large city in Perú. I asked our photography guys to go to Tacna and take photos of the rabbit billboard." Petra turned to me. "Cati, the guys will make slides of this billboard. Can you use these slides in your first presentation? Prepare your presentation in questions. Our method of teaching is to let the participants speak for themselves. We try to encourage critical thinking."

The photography guys hung a white sheet on the wall for a screen and gave me a hand-controlled slide projector. When the group was seated I turned off the lights and slid the slide of the billboard in front of the light bulb. The large rabbit now became the focal point when the slide was projected onto the white sheet.

The women giggled.

I said, "The government has made this billboard to represent family planning. Do you think this is a helpful image for women?"

One woman raised her hand. "Rabbits are very good for making rabbit stew."

Another added, "Especially if you cook the rabbit in wine."

The women smothered their laughter behind their open palms. I knew this was embarrassment because of missing front teeth. Women from the Andes often had missing teeth as few could afford dentistry. They simply knocked out the rotten tooth with a rock.

Another woman gave her recipe for a rabbit dish.

I walked to the chalk board and wrote *the rabbit is good for cooking*. "What else is the rabbit good for besides cooking?"

A woman at the back said, "It's very productive."

Another round of laughter.

"Right." I wrote *productive* on the chalk board. "Anything else the rabbit is good for?"

After a few moments of pensive silence, I asked, "Who else is in this billboard besides the rabbit?"

"An Andean woman."

"Yeah. Above the rabbit in the right-hand corner."

I pointed to the Andean woman on the screen. "Why is there a picture of an Andean woman on this billboard?"

"Women want family planning," a participant said.

"Yes, they do. Is this woman responsible for planning the number of children she has?"

"Yes," said a couple of women.

"No," said a younger woman in her twenties. "Her partner too is responsible."

"Yeah, that's true. He has at least half of the responsibility."

Women nodded in agreement. Now there was an elevated level of agitation amidst the humour.

I asked the bombshell question. "And on this billboard who does the rabbit represent?"

Angrily they made the connection and said, "The Andean woman."

"That's right."

"But we are not rabbits!" a woman said emphatically.

I allowed the loud venting in Aymara before I said, "In the next presentation we'll explore this topic again. See you next week."

Chapter Thirty-Nine

## THE RABBIT BILLBOARD

"How many of you talked about the rabbit billboard with your partner, friend, neighbour?"

Every woman's hand in the classroom was raised. More women were present for this third hour than were registered in the sewing class. *This is good. The more women who object to this billboard, the better chance it'll be removed.* "Why would the government have approved this billboard? Have you heard of any other city with this billboard?"

"My sister in Cuzco said she saw the rabbit, and women there are as angry as we are here about it."

"It's also in Chiclayo and Trujillo," said another woman.

"I heard it's in Puno as well," came a voice in the corner.

"Do you think our president knows about this billboard?"

"He has to have seen it. It's near the airport. He travels on the highway to the airport. Doesn't he?"

"Maybe his darkened limousine windows didn't let him see it."

"Yeah, maybe he had something in his eye when the limousine passed the rabbit." More laughter. *These women are united and supporting one another.*

"Has the government before now encouraged family planning?"

"The government won't let us have an abortion in the hospital," a woman said tearfully. "Women have abortions in the doctor's house at night." *I wonder if she's speaking from experience?*

"Many women haemorrhage and even die after these backstreet abortions."

"Sí, but what other alternative is there for us who have too many children?" *These comments represent their harsh reality.*

"Could pregnancy be prevented as opposed to ending a pregnancy?" I asked.

The younger woman spoke again, "Last week I went to the clinic in the pueblo joven because my Miguel was sick. The doctor treated him quickly then told me he could examine me for cancer of..." she hesitated, "my uterus? He said he'd take a swab and send it away. I agreed. But when I came home and peed, I felt a string hanging down. My husband says the doctor put something in me to stop me from getting pregnant. Is this true?"

"It sounds like the doctor inserted an IUD," I said. "Which will probably prevent you from getting pregnant. But it is wrong he did this without your consent or knowledge."

"My husband said he heard that the American president told our president to control Peruvian women's fertility. Is this why we have the rabbit billboard?"

"Who wants to answer this question?"

The answers came fast: "The United States should mind their own business."

"We're too dependent on United States."

"They're jealous because Peruvian women are more fertile than American women."

I noticed Petra standing by the door listening to the discussion. At a lull, she said, "Before we close for tonight, I'd like to share with you some news that I received today from a women's group in Lima. They have written a letter which will be sent to the ministers asking for the rabbit billboards to be removed as they are offensive to women. Attached to the letter is a petition of over a million signatures so far. I'll leave this sheet of paper on the table. If you'd like to add your signature and Libreta Tributaria (tax card number), please do. The goal is to have women's signatures from every corner of Perú. Please tell others, women and men, they may come to the centre to sign this petition."

(Happily I can share with you that every rabbit billboard in the country was removed as a result of the pressure on the government from los clubes de madres.)

A few days after this presentation I was visiting Joanna and her family when I heard over a loudspeaker: "Women, come to the clinic for free testing."

I asked Joanna, "What's this about?"

"Some doctors are here from Lima with their nurses. They're visiting all the clinics. It's a free pap test campaign for cervical cancer."

*Oh Lord, these doctors and nurses are inserting IUDs while doing a pap test. If they even do the pap test.*

"Sorry Joanna, I can't stay. I must head back to the centre. I'll return tomorrow."

I sped to the centre on my orange motor scooter, catching Juan Luis just as he was going into a meeting.

"Cati, you look anxious. What's up?"

"Doctors and nurses from Lima are in the three pueblo joven clinics putting IUDs in women without their consent. They advertise the service from the back of a pick-up truck with a loudspeaker, calling it a pap test."

Juan Luis frowned. "Thank you for telling me, Cati. This is a human rights violation. I'll see to it immediately."

In the midst of the rabbit billboard campaign and the pap test campaign, we sisters received the English edition of the November 1983 *Reader's Digest*. In this edition was an article titled "Today's Contraceptives: What's New/What's Best," which described the different types of contraceptives. It also detailed the risks and dangers associated with each contraceptive and stated who should not use them.

Our women's group held an emergency meeting.

"So, this is where the IUDs have suddenly come from," stated Lucia.

"And now they're wanting to use them on the poorest women in our pueblo."

Petra said, "I searched in the November edition of *Selecciones* (the Peruvian edition of *Reader's Digest*) for this article that Cati tells us was in the English *Reader's Digest* but I couldn't find it."

"Would you like me to show the original article with a translation to the women in the sewing class?"

The response was unanimous.

"Yes, women need to be informed of the risks and dangers," said one member.

"And who should use or not use the different types of contraceptives," I added.

Pablo, from the team's newspaper section made the slide of the Reader's Digest with Spanish translation. He shared, "We're making a cartoon about this article in our weekly magazine. The more we can educate the public on what is happening to our most vulnerable female population, the better."

"Thanks, Pablo, for your ongoing support."

"You be careful, Cati. Don't forget Shining Path (Sendero Luminoso) is infiltrating our classes."

"I'll try be careful but I can't be silent either. No member on our team is silent about human rights violations."

Not only did the traditional and official Catholic church in Perú frown on priests and sisters supporting the poor in their struggles, but so too did Sendero Luminoso oppose our teaching in los pueblos jovenes. They categorized us as colonialists and capitalists.

Pablo's concern intensified my awareness of the Shining Path movement. They were a Peruvian Maoist guerrilla group determined to overthrow the government. Their founder, Abimael Guzman, promised a new shining path to freedom for the poor. He originally believed in community (communism) which meant he was opposed to capitalism – either in the form of an American government or the Roman Catholic Church. This left us sisters and priests who opted to live with the poor in a precarious situation. We had no protection from either side.

On national television a reporter asked a Shining Path leader, "Up until now you have killed many members of the Catholic Church but you haven't killed any of their representatives. How come?"

We knew that he meant bishops, priests and sisters. We sisters listened as the Shining Path leader behind his black Balaclava facemask said, "We're keeping them for our dessert."

My blood ran cold. We turned the TV off.

Our leadership team sister asked, "Who would like me to list their name with the Canadian Embassy in Lima? Anyone whose name is listed with the embassy will be evacuated if there's more violence from the Shining Path or an overthrow of the government."

Only the newly arrived sisters wanted to be evacuated in case of emergency. The rest of us who had lived in Perú for more than ten and fifteen years didn't want to be evacuated.

"It sends a wrong message to the people," one sister said. "It says our commitment is contingent on our safety."

Sister Maureen said, "Jesus knew His life was on the line but he didn't abandon His flock. I want to stay."

After a pause, I said, "I agree with both sisters. Like them, I'm here with the people in safe and unsafe times."

It was a tense and unpredictable time, but the government wasn't overthrown and none of our sisters were evacuated.

※ ※ ※

PRIOR TO THE PRESIDENTIAL ELECTIONS of 1984-85, I stayed with some American sisters in Arequipa for my weekend off. On my arrival I said, "I had the weirdest experience on the bus coming here. I was in the third row by the window when the bus suddenly came to an abrupt stop. A jeep blocked the road in front of our bus. Armed masked men got out of their jeep and pointed long guns at us. Two of them ascended the stairs. Civil guards walked slowly up the centre aisle from the back of the bus with their guns visible. When the masked armed men saw the civil guards, they stepped backwards down the stairs."

Sister Nancy who had been listening intently said, "I bet they did. Those masked men were the Shining Path. They're stealing Peruvian documents to prevent Peruvians from voting. I'm glad the civil guards were on the bus."

"I am too."

*Thank You, Jesus, for protecting me and everyone on the bus.*

Chapter Forty

# THE FISHERMEN'S SYNDICATE

At our Thursday morning meeting Petra said, "The fishermen's syndicate has invited our team to participate in their week of celebrations. Juan Luis told them we could do a presentation on a health issue. They suggested the presentation be on tuberculosis."

"What does the group think about our participation in the fishermen's celebrations?"

"Any educational opportunity is welcomed," said one team member.

"Especially if we get to educate men for a change!" humorously said another.

Petra smiled and asked, "Are you game to take on this new challenge, Cati?"

"What woman doesn't want to work with men?" I said jokingly, with an exaggerated wink. "But I'd prefer to do a presentation on family planning than tuberculosis. It's too good an opportunity to miss to help men understand their role in family planning. Women continue to tell me their partners say, 'You're the one who carries the baby. It's up to you to do something if you don't want to get pregnant. Don't blame me for getting you pregnant.' It's a macho mentality."

A co-worker at the table agreed and said, "Yes, a presentation on family planning would be much more in keeping with our goal to liberate women from oppression."

"I can't do this presentation in one evening," I said. "I'd need five evenings to cover this topic completely. And I'd want a Peruvian nurse midwife from the hospital with me."

Petra hesitated then said, "Okay, I'll mention this proposal to Juan Luis and see if he will present it to the syndicate representative."

Juan Luis and the representative negotiated until they reached a compromise. We'd have four consecutive evenings for a presentation on family planning. Raquel agreed to be co-presenter and we met to draft a plan for how we'd present the information.

"Raquel, I have to be careful teaching the artificial methods as most know I'm a sister."

"Yes, I understand. It puts you in a difficult position. How about if I teach and invite you to share your knowledge? Then you aren't directly teaching what the Catholic church is adamantly against."

"Yeah, that could work. On the final night I'll share about the *Reader's Digest* article and the recent pap test campaign."

"That should lead to questions and a heated discussion," commented Raquel.

"Hope so… that's the point!"

At 7:00 p.m. on the first night the fishermen seated themselves on the long wooden benches. The women leaned against the side and back walls, their babies snuggled to their breasts. There were approximately 400 men and 100 women in the hall.

"Welcome everyone to these four nights on family planning," I said. "I ask you to refrain from asking questions until the fourth and final night. The last two hours on that night will be for your questions."

Raquel stepped forward. "Cati and I are speaking as nurse midwives, as health care providers. Our teaching won't be affiliated with any religion or religious beliefs. We'll tell you impartially the pros and cons of each method of family planning."

Over the first two nights Raquel explained the effects and side effects of oral contraceptives, injectable contraceptives, condoms, and IUDs. On the third night I showed a slide of the female anatomy and asked, "Which female organ produces the egg?"

"The ovary," a male participant said.

"Correct. The ovaries determine a woman's fertility." I explained in detail how the natural method of family planning is an alternate way to space pregnancies or to avoid a pregnancy. "The natural method is not 100% reliable. No method is." I went on. "What is the name of the tube along which the egg travels when it leaves the ovary?"

There was mumbling but no one answered.

"The fallopian tubes." I pointed to each fallopian tube on the projected drawing. "These tubes are surgically cut when a woman is sterilized. A couple must be very sure they don't want to have any more children before this surgery is done."

I replaced the female anatomy slide with a male anatomy slide. The discomfort in the hall was tangible. I pretended not to notice and proceeded with explaining a vasectomy.

As planned, on the final night I shared the article on contraceptives in the English edition of the *Reader's Digest* and told the fishermen that the article had been omitted from *Selecciones*.

Raquel added, "Cati and I have also read another article stating that Provera and the copper IUD, that are no longer approved in the United States, have recently arrived in one-ton containers in Callao and other Peruvian ports."

Once this shocking statement settled over the atmosphere I said, "As Raquel mentioned on the first night, our responsibility as health care providers is to educate. Now, you have the information. It's the responsibility of every couple to choose which method is best for them. It's no one else's decision but yours as a couple to make. Thank you for your attention during these four nights. These next two hours are for your questions and for discussion."

I took a seat at the side of the stage and Raquel remained at the microphone.

For the first hour Raquel answered questions professionally and in layman's language. Her explanations were well received by the fishermen. Then, at the beginning of the second hour a fisherman stood up from the bench he was sitting on and said, "This question is for Hermana Catalina."

As soon as I heard him addressing me as 'sister' I knew it wasn't going to be good. I walked to the microphone.

"You are a sister," he said. "How can you teach us these artificial methods when the Pope says we aren't to use contraceptives?"

A dead silence filled the hall. I could feel the heat rising from the soles of my feet and my heart pounded. But in a calm strong voice I said, "First let me remind you we made it clear we weren't speaking in the name of any religion but rather as professional nurse midwives. But I'll answer your question. The Pope also says that Catholics are to attend Sunday Mass. I've never seen any of you men at Sunday Mass. It seems hypocritical to quote the Pope when it's convenient to do so but not follow all of his recommendations."

I took a slow deep breath. I hadn't prepared for what I was about to say next. The words flowed articulately and effortlessly as if I wasn't the speaker. "If I should die tonight," I said, "I've no fear of facing God or of being judged for trying to protect women by teaching them about birth control methods. I don't believe God is going to have any problem with women using contraceptives to protect themselves from husbands who rape them in their drunken state."

There was complete silence in the hall of 500 people. "But I think God will have a very hard time with men who have children in several different cities in Perú and refuse to give these children their surname. You know, as I know, a child without a legitimate surname is not permitted to attend school. If I can help women prevent a pregnancy in these kind of situations through education, I'll continue to teach with God as my witness." I looked straight at the participant who had posed the question. "Have I answered your question, sir?"

He simply remained seated and nodded his head affirmatively.

Before leaving the hall, many women came and hugged me. It was rewarding.

Raquel said, "Wow, you sure socked it to them. Good for you, Cati."

"Thanks. In the gospel of Matthew Jesus says, 'I'm sending you out like sheep among wolves.'"

Raquel interrupted and said, "Yeah, he was a wolf alright trying to embarrass and trap you."

"Let me tell you the rest of what Jesus said. He said, 'Be on your guard... do not worry about what to say or how to say it... the words will be given to you. The Spirit of the Father will speak through you.' I've never felt this before tonight, Raquel. It was like someone was speaking to these men through me."

"That's amazing. What an experience."

"Yes. Thank you, Raquel, for all your support and help. You did a great job in your presentation. Please come to our Thursday meeting and share with Petra and our team how it was for you."

"Okay. See you at the meeting."

An hour after the fishermen's syndicate presentation, Juan Luis came looking for me. "Cati, I heard that you spoke very strongly to the fishermen. We don't need to upset them even if we're speaking the truth. Perú is in a stressful political time with the Shining Path. As director I'd be the one taken. I prefer not to be jailed if I can help it."

"Sorry," I said. "I'll be more diplomatic."

He raised his eyebrows in his typical fashion and said, "Good!"

Many years after I left Perú, I learned that Father Juan Luis Moyano Walker S.J. had been a political prisoner in Argentina's Dirty War years and had been tortured. No wonder he cautioned me to be more diplomatic. For me, to have known Juan Luis, who died from a brain tumour in 2006, was to have known Jesus Christ in human form on this Earth. May he rest in peace.

Chapter Forty-One

# AN ALTIPLANO WORKSHOP

*Querida Hermana Catalina,*
 *My name is Sonya. Raquel told me she loved working with you and recommended I invite you to accompany me in a workshop on Responsible Parenthood. I need to do this workshop for my thesis. I'm studying midwifery. If you're available to come to Putina July 22-26, 1985 I'd be very grateful.*
 *Because Putina is on the opposite side of Lake Titicaca from Puno, I'll stay in the convent in Moho which is a two-hour walk from Putina. You probably could stay at this convent as well. I'll meet you in Puno. We'll take the boat across Lake Titicaca together. The workshop will be for four days, six hours a day. On Monday 22nd we'll go to Putina to introduce ourselves to the community. We'll start the workshop on Tuesday. I hope you'll agree to accompany me in this workshop. I'll look forward to hearing from you.*
 *Your colleague Sonya*

*Dear Sonya,*
 *It's a joy to hear you're studying midwifery. We need Peruvian*

*midwives. I happily accept your invitation to do this workshop in Putina. I've never been in the Altiplano or seen Lake Titicaca. Can't wait to see the Highlands of the Andes and have the experience of crossing this magnificent lake with you. I'll meet you in Puno on Sunday July 21st.*

*Until then,*
*Hermana Catalina*

WITH GREAT ANTICIPATION I TOOK the seven-hour bus ride from our fishing city on the southern border to Puno. I arrived at dawn to see Lake Titicaca in full view from the bus window. A few hours later Sonya and I made the boat crossing on Lake Titicaca from Puno to Moho. This immense lake surrounded by the Andes was more beautiful than any photos I had seen. After a good night's sleep in the convent, the next morning we started our two-hour trek from Moho to Putina.

On the dusty uneven pathways we shared with cows, bulls, sheep and shepherd boys, Sonya and I confided our hopes and fears for the workshop.

"I'm afraid these Aymara men and women may reject me because I look like a city slicker," Sonya said. "I lack their high cheek bones, I can't speak Aymara, and my Spanish is from upper-class education."

"Don't worry, Sonya. I doubt if these men and women will judge us. They'll probably be happy we care to come to their remote village."

We sat on a rock admiring the expansive chacras (farmlands) while drinking water from our thermoses. "My biggest fear," I said, "is for our workshop to be rejected on religious grounds. The Aymara people may not be practising Catholics but they adhere to a traditional Catholicism the Spaniards brought to them centuries ago."

"That's a valid point. And family planning is a counter-cultural topic." After a brief pause, she said, "We'll have to charm them over!"

As we neared the village we saw the colourful red, yellow, turquoise of the Aymara women's shawls and flared skirts against the green and brown landscape. Two men holding crude tiling instruments came to meet us.

One said in Spanish, "Welcome, nurses. We've expected you and are happy to have you with us."

The younger man said, "I'm Agustino and I'll be your interpreter for the week."

"Thank you, Agustino."

The four of us walked toward a semi-cycle of women and children seated on the ground in the shade.

Sonya addressed the women. "Hola Señoras. Soy Sonya."

Agustino translated and the women clapped.

I said, "Soy Cati." It seemed easier than saying Hermana Catalina.

We sat on the ground with them. Sonya turned to Agustino. "Could you please make sure everyone understands this workshop is for couples only and no couple can join the group once the workshop starts on Tuesday."

After this was translated, I said, "We'll show you pictures to help you to see what we're saying. Do you have any questions?"

They talked in Aymara among themselves and then someone asked, "Can the children be with us? The children like pictures."

"No. Not during the workshop. But if the children are really good for the elders who mind them, we'll show them a special movie on the final day before we leave."

They clapped in approval. We joined in the clapping as we stood and said our goodbyes.

The first image was on the white sheet when the eleven couples, including Agustino and his wife, entered the classroom-sized adobe room. The women hugged Sonya and me while the men gave us firm handshakes.

Once they took a seat on the wooden benches, Sonya asked, "Can anyone tell me what is in this picture?"

A man said, "I see a man and a woman looking at one another."

Another man said, "I see the man and woman holding hands while looking at one another."

This was our ice breaker slide to encourage participation. Sonya and I noted the women's lack of participation. We hoped this would change.

By the end of the first day the couples presented their drawings of the female reproductive system. Except their drawings looked nothing like the images on the slides. Each couple's drawing depicted a bull's head.

"Can you explain your drawing to me?" I asked a woman.

She pointed to the bull's neck and said, "This is the vagina."

Her husband pointed to the head and said, "This is the uterus. And the horns are the fallopian tubes."

The woman pointed and said, "We drew the ovaries here under the horns."

I was overjoyed with their explanation. "Now, as a couple you'll be able to teach your children sex education."

The eleven couples were proud of their drawings and eager to learn more in the following days.

In the morning of day two we showed slides of the male reproductive system.

Sonya asked, "Which is the most important organ in the male reproductive system?"

They laughed but didn't answer the question.

Sonya smirked. "No, the penis is not the correct answer."

Couples snickered.

Sonya pointed to the prostate gland on the image and said, "Without this gland a man is infertile."

The couples became serious and began to ask questions; they clearly wanted to understand how the male reproductive system functioned. The plan for the afternoon session was for couples to draw as they had the previous day. Sonya and I were curious to see what their drawings would look like. During lunch we sat outdoors with the women at a long wooden table while the men sat at another long table. This is a typical Aymara custom for men and women to sit separately.

Ten minutes before resuming the afternoon session Agustino said to Sonya, "Señor Ugarte wants to join the workshop with his wife. I told him no one is permitted to join if they weren't present on the first day. He demands to talk with you."

"I'll talk with Cati, then we'll both talk with Señor Ugarte."

Agustino's voice betrayed annoyance. "Señor Ugarte knew this workshop was for couples but he refused to join when his wife wanted to come. It is his way of controlling her. The rest of us men make decisions with our wives. I'm told he became jealous when he heard some men sharing their new knowledge."

"Let me speak to Cati," Sonya said calmly. "She's older and has much experience. I'm sure she'll be able to reason with Señor Ugarte."

I suggested to Sonya that she approach Señor Ugarte. "Tell him it's too late to join this workshop but we'd be happy to return to do another workshop for him and his wife along with other couples."

She did so and he walked away silently. We assumed he'd think about our suggestion and we'd hear from him in the near future.

Our assumption was wrong. After lunch Sonya and I watched our eleven couples flinging their arms about and speaking loudly in Aymara. The husbands and wives were in some kind of disagreement. Then the eleven women stomped into the makeshift classroom while their husbands remained outdoors.

"What's happening?" I asked Agustino. "Did their husbands tell them to go inside?"

"No. The women say they are continuing the workshop and their husbands have to choose whether to support them or Señor Ugarte. Señor Ugarte asked the couples to boycott the workshop because he and his wife couldn't participate."

When the eleven men slowly followed their wives into the room, we knew whom they supported.

Sonya said, "Thank you. Please do your drawings as a couple. Cati and I are here to assist you if you need help or have questions."

On the third day the artificial methods of birth control and tubal ligation were discussed. Nothing was rejected on religious grounds as I feared might happen but we were treated to a 'macho' perspective. A man said, "If my wife can't get pregnant how will I know if she's faithful to me?"

Other men muttered, "Yeah, how will we know?"

"Too many women die in childbirth," Sonya said. "The high mortality rate is due to numerous pregnancies. You decide if you want to protect your partner or have orphaned children." This explanation squelched any remaining skepticism.

As promised, we showed a movie to the children on the last evening. And we surprised the couples with a certificate. This was an emotional moment as none of the participants had ever received a certificate before. For Sonya and I, the certificate symbolized our affectionate bond with the eleven Aymara couples in Putina.

## Chapter Forty-Two

## YAVARI

The sisters in Moho befriended me during the week Sonya and I stayed with them. In February of '86, Sister Gloria phoned and asked, "Sister Kathleen, the couples in my family catechesis program would like to learn about family planning. These young couples don't want to have eight and ten children like their parents. If you agree to do a workshop with them, would the second week in April work for you? The celebration of Las Cruces (The Crosses) begins on May 3rd and continues for most of the month. I think it would be best to hold the workshop before the festivities begin."

"April would work for me but I can't make a commitment until I run this by my sisters."

"Of course. I understand. I hope you can stay for the festivities. They're spectacular."

"Yes, I've heard about them and have seen photos of the locals and tourists dancing in the streets. I love the altiplano music. God willing I'll return to Moho in April. Thanks for inviting me to work with the young couples."

"By the way," Sister Gloria added, "you won't need an interpreter as these young people speak Spanish."

"That's great. I'll call you next Monday, okay?"

"That'll be fine. Talk to you then. Chou."

"Chou."

My community of sisters agreed I'd do the workshop in Moho. Sister Gloria met me in Puno on Friday April 11th.

After welcoming me she said, "I've been stuck here in Puno since March 3rd. We've had torrential rains for months and there's no way to get back to Moho. Lake Titicaca has flooded homes and lands for miles around. All the crops are wiped out. Mud is everywhere. The locals say the lake has risen 8 feet, twice the normal for our rainy season."

"On the coast we heard that Lake Titicaca had flooded but I'd no idea it was this bad. When do you think we'll be able to get to Moho?"

"I've heard that they're going to take a British steamship, the *Yavari*, out of storage and see if it's seaworthy. Apparently, she's a 100-year-old ship that was retired a few years ago."

"Sounds risky. You're not thinking of us going on it, are you?" I asked in trepidation.

"After waiting for over a month I think I'm ready to take any mode of transportation!"

Three days later we saw the ship in the harbour and passengers boarding her. Sister Gloria, who was a tall, middle-aged English woman, said, "Vamos."

The ship was rusty, long and low with an upper and lower deck and a fat red stack behind a wheelhouse. The locals remained on the upper deck while Sister Gloria and I were ushered down a set of worn wooden stairs into an open area with portholes on either side. The only furniture to the left of the creaky stairs was a stationary wide wooden antique desk.

"WOW, how old do you think this desk is? I bet the ship's captain kept a logbook. I'm going to look for it."

"And when you finish looking for a logbook," Sister Gloria said, "you may want to look at your bed for the night!"

Lost in admiration I opened the deep bottom drawer and removed the heavy brown embossed logbook. "It has dates from the 1870s," I said. "How historical is this?"

Sister Gloria wasn't as enthralled as I was with the logbook. She merely acknowledged my jubilation with, "Yeah."

After I read the last entry on the lined yellow page, I looked at the slabs of dark wood suspended by metal arms above the port holes on both sides of the ship's belly.

"Take your pick," she said. "Do you want to be on the right or left side?"

"The left side."

I lay on my back and recalled stanzas from *The Rime of The Ancient Mariner* as waves pelted the porthole against my left shoulder. I prayed to the blessed Virgin Mary under her title *Star of the Sea* and asked her to guide our ship across Lake Titicaca in darkness.

In the morning when Sister Gloria and I ascended the stairs the bright sun on the blue waves welcomed us. On deck we staggered among the crowd of men, women and children who squatted on their ponchos. The aroma of strong coffee from open thermoses hit my nostrils and provoked a nauseous sensation of sea sickness. I tried to ignore the up and down water as I stepped over legs and ponchos in an effort to find a seat somewhere on this crowded deck.

Seeing that I was about to lose my balance, a seasoned campesino said, "Sister, please take my seat when I stand." He held my elbow firmly until I was seated on the narrow wooden bench along the ship's flank.

"Thank you, Señor." I said nervously. "I don't have much sailing experience."

He smiled. "Normally Lake Titicaca isn't this full and rough. We farmers have lost our crops to the flooding. Many have lost their homes as well as their crops."

After commiserating with him I asked, "What is the main crop you sow?"

"Mostly potatoes, yucca and corn."

His eyes watered as he remembered his lost crops. He excused himself by tipping his sombrero and turned to face his wife on the bench in front of me.

My eyes grew heavy as the strong sun baked the deck. My thighs slid sideways on the bench tilting my right shoulder to a right angle with the ship's uneven hard edge. I tucked the blue nylon anorak, my 1971 going-away present from the sisters in England, into the hollow below my neck. The anorak cushioned my head and within minutes I was in dreamland... only to be woken when a forceful wave smacked my face and took my anorak! In disbelief I watched my blue nylon anorak float on top of the water until it was lost in the wake and swept under Lake Titicaca's surface. Never to be seen again.

In Moho I witnessed the devastation left behind by the floods. The once-smooth graded dirt roads were now bumpy muddy mounds, with rocks and driftwood. Lake weed was the only visible sign of life in the farmers' fields. There were no cows, horses, sheep or vehicles to be seen. The government and various religious groups had set-up temporary shelters for those who had lost their homes.

Sister Gloria looked very sad. "Sister Kathleen," she said, "since my catechesis couples are unable to get here for your workshop, would you like to accompany me tomorrow when I visit some farmers and their families?"

"Certainly. I'd love to go."

"Are you a good walker?"

"Yes, I think so."

"Because it'll be a twelve-hour trek on rough terrain. Six hours to the farthest chacra and six hours back home. I want to leave at 5 a.m. Are you still interested?"

"Yes."

We left the house in the 5 a.m. darkness with knapsacks on our backs, wearing heavy waterproof boots, wide-brim hats, and carrying flashlights in our hands. I did my best to maintain Sister Gloria's rhythmic strides as we ascended. Our starting altitude was 3,812 metres.

Periodically she'd look back to make sure I was behind her. Speaking wasn't an option. The goal was to preserve oxygen given our limited lung capacity. We lacked the barrel-shaped lungs of the locals born in high altitudes.

At approximately 3,901 metres I stopped walking. Sister Gloria returned to my side. "Kathleen, are you okay?"

"Oh, I'm admiring the beautiful twisting colours between the canyon and the immense ocean of sky."

"What did you say?"

"I'm admiring the tinsel everywhere. It's so beautiful. Like a Christmas tree. Except this tinsel is in colour."

She poured a black coffee with honey into the lid of her thermos, handed it to me, and said, "Drink this. Your blood sugar and possibly blood pressure have dropped."

We sat on a huge smooth rock to drink the sweetened black coffee and share a hearty roast beef sandwich. Once my tummy was full, the coloured tinsel disappeared and never returned. I felt disappointed yet grateful for the experience of this visual hallucination.

The Aymara men and women with their ruddy weather-beaten

complexions welcomed Sister Gloria with open arms. It was obvious they loved her like one of their own. The children excitedly danced around in a circle holding onto their mothers' woollen flared skirts.

"Let me introduce you to Hermana Catalina," Sister Gloria said. "She's visiting with us for a few weeks. She'll stay for La Fiesta de las Cruces."

"Bienvenida, Hermana Catalina."

"Gracias."

They were happy to report that the potato starters that Sister Gloria had given them had taken root and promised a good harvest. The farmlands above Lake Titicaca had been more affected by the constant low clouds than by the floods. Samuel, the last farmer we visited, shared a picturesque image of their nightlife in the highlands.

"Each farmer takes his turn in keeping the campfires burning all night to protect our crops from the low clouds." The smoke prevented frost from forming on the leaves.

The optimism and collaborative spirit of this farming community lightened our hearts as we descended the uneven pathways.

Chapter Forty-Three

## CHILDBIRTH IN THE CONVENT

Now that you, readers of my memoir, have journeyed with me to Lake Titicaca, I'll keep the promise I made to you when I was a student midwife and Dr. Bhatt taught me how to suture. I told you this new skill would save a young woman's life. Now I'll share with you how this happened, though it's not an easy story for me to tell.

When Sister Gloria and I returned exhausted from our twelve-hour trek, Sister Sarilyn met us. "Doctor Acuna from the government clinic came this afternoon. He heard that you, Sister Kathleen, are a nurse midwife and would like to speak with you. He said he'd return this evening at 7:00 p.m."

He was punctual. When I opened the door, he spoke hastily before any introductions were established. "My wife and I have to take the *Yavari* to Puno and from there we fly to Lima."

He was dressed in a heavy black coat and sombrero. I estimated him to be in his late fifties. He didn't share what was behind the urgency of his travel nor did I ask.

He said, "I have a primigravida who is due to give birth while

I'm away. I'd like to know if you would attend to this birth in my absence."

"I don't have my maternity instruments with me."

"There's everything you'll need for a delivery in the clinic," he assured me. "I'll leave you the keys."

"Is there Lignocaine and suturing thread in case I need to do an episiotomy?"

"Of course. You'll find everything in the cabinet. You can deliver Luisa in the clinic. I told her to go there when she starts labour and to send Jaime, her husband, to the convent to get you. Sorry for the urgency but I must leave now. Thank you for helping me out in this situation."

He turned and left before I could refuse or agree to accept this maternity case. All the *'what ifs'* rushed into my consciousness. *What if* this woman can't delivery and needs a forceps delivery or a C-section? *What if* baby needs oxygen? Is there any oxygen in the clinic? *What if* there's a post-partum haemorrhage? *The Puno hospital is on the other side of Lake Titicaca. And there aren't any medical evacuation airplanes in the Andes. Oh God, help me.*

Before this avalanche of worries, I had been physically tired from the day's journey but now I was emotionally overwhelmed. When I didn't return to the community room, Sister Sarilyn came to look for me. She found me sitting on a large bean bag on the chapel's concrete floor with my back against the adobe wall looking up at the crucifix.

"Is everything okay, Sister Kathleen?" Sister whispered. "What did Dr. Acuna have to say?"

I shook my head in bewilderment. Neither of us spoke until we left the chapel.

The young woman's labour started in the evening two days later which gave me time to recuperate and prepare myself mentally to attend her birth. Jaime came to the convent as planned and said, "My wife is at the clinic. She has pain."

"I'll come, Jaime."

In the darkness of 5:30 p.m., we walked by flashlight along the dry rutted road. Sensing Jaime's stress from his heavy footfalls, I tried to reassure him. "Don't worry, your wife will be fine. I've delivered many babies."

"I'm praying to our Lady of Guadeloupe," he said.

When we reached the clinic, Luisa was leaning against the grey adobe wall.

"I'm Sister Kathleen. I'll help you deliver your baby, Luisa."

She smiled and said, "Gracias." She was taller than most Aymara women, which I evaluated as positive. *With that height she probably has an adequate pelvis and should have a reasonably easy birth.*

I unlocked the metal door. "When did your contractions start, Luisa?"

"Two hours ago. They're coming every twenty minutes."

The clinic was damp and dark. I searched for a light switch. Found one on the far wall. With a flick of the switch electricity entered the nude light bulb dangling over the hard lacerated-leather examination table. There were no sheets or blankets. *Perhaps they're in the cabinet.* No such luck. The cabinet contained an enema can, a couple of glass measuring jars, a blood-pressure cuff and unsterilized glass syringes. In the cabinet drawer I found two rusty forceps.

*Oh Lord! There're no delivery instruments, suturing thread, local anaesthetic... nothing. Did this doctor clear off and take everything with him? Or was there never anything here to start with? Kathleen, stop wasting your energy focusing on what isn't.*

I turned to the couple and said, "I'm going to the convent to ask the sisters if I may borrow sheets and blankets. I'll return pronto."

After Sisters Gloria and Sarilyn listened to my account of the clinic's condition they said, "Bring the woman here. There're two beds in your room. You'll have good lighting, warmth and hot water here. It'll be more comfortable for both of you."

"Good idea. It'll be safer here. Thank you. I'll return with Luisa shortly."

In the semi-dark room Luisa laboured throughout the night while I dozed off and on in the bed a few feet from her. At midnight she was 6 centimetres dilated with waters intact. Baby's heart rate remained strong and regular at 125 beats per minute. I anticipated she'd deliver somewhere around 5:00 a.m. *Mother of God, please allow Luisa to delivery her baby with no complications.*

Luisa breathed deeply with her contractions. Her composure was admirable in this strange environment alone without her husband or mother.

At 4:37 a.m. she yelled when a strong contraction caused warm water to gush down her inner thighs.

I leaped from my bed. "This is good, Luisa. Baby is ready to come out. May I examine you and listen to baby's heart?"

"Yes, Sister. Help me."

Baby's heartbeat was strong and regular. The cervix was fully dilated and baby's head was low in the pelvis. But I was alarmed to feel an irregular raised edge on baby's head. *How can there possibly be overlapping of the skull bones when the water has just broken? Overlapping happens when the water ruptures early and labour is prolonged. Luisa's labour has been short and her water remained intact until now.*

Luisa bore down and pushed forcibly with each contraction.

A knock came at the bedroom door, which quickly opened.

Sisters Gloria and Sarilyn brought the forceps to me after removing the rust and sterilizing them in boiling water.

"Can we watch baby being born?" Sister Gloria asked.

Luisa nodded as she clenched and bore down again. Baby's head was visible in the bloody, stained mucous of the vagina. *Should I do an episiotomy because of this ridge on baby's head? But I can't... I have no surgical scissors, no lignocaine and no suturing thread.*

When baby's head crowned, I saw four long fingers clinging to the head. Luisa gave her final push and her baby girl lay on the bed with her right hand on top of her head. I said out loud, to no one in particular, "I've seen many photos in midwifery books of baby's presentation at birth but I've never seen a photo of a baby presenting with its hand on top of its head. This is one for the books."

While Luisa held her daughter, I asked Sisters Gloria and Sarilyn, "Do you have a sewing basket?"

"Yes."

"Can you bring me strong thread and a curved needle?"

"I think so," Sister Sarilyn said. "Why?"

"I need you to boil a curved needle and some thick thread in a pan of water for five minutes. Luisa has a small tear and I need to suture it."

With a horrified look Sister Sarilyn said, "That's barbarous. You can't suture this woman's tear with a furniture needle and thread."

"It'd be barbarous for me to let her lose blood from the tear and for the wound to get infected because I didn't suture without an anaesthetic or proper suturing thread," I said. "Please boil both and bring them to me asap. I have to do what I have to do."

The two sisters left. Luisa continued to cuddle her newborn.

She said she couldn't wait for Jaime to meet his daughter. Sister Gloria returned with the sterilized needle and thread.

"Luisa," I said, "you've a small tear that has to be sutured. I'm sorry but I have to put five sutures in. We'll count them together… here goes."

Luisa yelled when I inserted the needle for the first time. Sister Sarilyn returned and took baby from the room. Sister Gloria held Luisa's head to her bosom.

I counted out loud. "Two more pricks, Luisa, we're nearly done. I cringed on inserting the needle but maintained the moderate thread tension Dr. Bhatt had suggested I use to promote healing and reduce swelling. All five sutures lined themselves up evenly. Sister Gloria gave Luisa a hot facecloth to freshen her tearful face before Sister Sarilyn brought baby back in to her for feeding.

## Chapter Forty-Four

# FIESTA DE LAS CRUCES

Luisa and Baby Mercedes remained in the convent for ten days following delivery. The relationship between Luisa and me was strained because of the uncompromising counter-cultural expectations I had for her post-natal care. Four hours after she delivered, I insisted she get out of bed. "Walk to the bathroom, pee, and have a shower."

"A woman shouldn't leave her bed for the first week after giving birth," she said. "I'll pee in a bedpan. I don't need to get washed. I need to keep my poncho on and keep warm in bed." *There's no medical facility on this side of Lake Titicaca. She and I are in this predicament together and I'm determined we'll survive it.*

"Luisa," I said, "here in the altiplano many women die after childbirth and many newborns die in their first week of life. I don't want you or your baby on the mortality list. You need to trust me."

She eased herself to the edge of the bed then slowly made her way to the bathroom. I smiled when I heard her pee. I straightened her sheets and fluffed her pillows, then knocked on the ajar door. "Here, let me turn on the water for you."

Her body pulled back when she saw the water spitting from the water spout high on the shower wall. I could see she was ready to bolt.

"Luisa, the water is warm. Ease your way in. Wet your arms first. That's good. Wet your legs. You're doing well."

Reluctantly she stepped into the crude concrete shower stall.

"Now stand with your back to the water."

She remained in the shower longer than I had anticipated she would. *This is good. We've gotten over our first hurdle. I can use this accomplishment to convince her to conquer other new challenges. And there're going to be many.*

"Luisa, you must clean the base of baby's umbilical cord with alcohol twice a day. Let me show you how."

Her 22-year-old frame recoiled with the thought of cleaning the stump. *She probably thinks this is my job as a midwife. No way. My job is to teach her how to care for her baby.*

"Now let me watch you, Luisa." I stood to one side and observed her gentleness with Baby Mercedes.

"Am I doing it right?"

"Perfectly. Do you think baby would like to be put to the breast before laying her down?"

"Yes. It's time for another feed. She's a good feeder."

"I've noticed. She feeds well in your secure embrace. You're a great mother, Luisa."

She smiled as she pushed her long thick black braid over her shoulder exposing her breast for Mercedes. Before I left the room to give her some privacy I said, "Don't forget to wash your nipples after feeding and apply the cream to prevent them from cracking."

"Yes. Thank you, Sister Kathleen, I'll do it as you've taught me."

Jaime came every evening with flowers picked from the hillside for Luisa and Mercedes. Luisa combed and re-braided her hair before his visit as she did before her mother's visit at lunch hour. Her mother brought a two-course meal in pots wrapped in newspaper and a heavy woollen poncho. First, she'd spread the newspaper on the tiled floor between Luisa's bed and mine. Then she'd meticulously place the poncho on top of the newspaper before allocating the pots round the poncho's perimeter. She brought soup bowls, dinner plates and teacups along with the pots. Luisa remained seated in bed while her mother served her. Between servings her mother squatted on the poncho on the floor. Sometimes I squatted beside her and enjoyed her home-cooked Aymara food. Especially the semolina chicken soup ladened with fresh crushed cilantro and the garlic rice eaten with my closed fingers.

Every morning and evening I prepared a sitz bath for Luisa. The first time I told her to lower her buttocks into the basin she objected strongly. "Water has parasites," she said. "They'll enter my vagina."

"It's okay. Just sit in the hot salty water for fifteen minutes. The salt will heal your wound. The quicker your wound heals the sooner I can remove the sutures and the more comfortable you'll feel."

After experiencing relief in the sutured area from the sitz bath, she said she'd prepare her own basin twice a day.

The biggest challenge for Luisa came when I said, "Mercedes has jaundice. The fastest way to eliminate jaundice is to lay baby nude in the sunshine."

"I do what you suggest for me, Sister Kathleen, but I won't let you place my baby in the sunshine nude."

I decided to appeal to her intellect rather than feed into her raw emotions. "Do you know the harm jaundice can do if it's allowed to progress?"

"No. Won't it go away on its own?"

"Luisa, the quicker it's eliminated the healthier your baby will be. If this pigment deepens it could affect Mercedes' brain."

Tears welled up in Luisa's eyes.

I hugged her. "If we treat baby now with an increased water intake and sunshine no harm will come to her."

Early morning sun shone through the kitchen windows. Mercedes lay nude on a towel on the kitchen table with her eyes covered. Luisa held her hand while baby sunbathed in her sleep.

On the tenth post-natal day Luisa and Mercedes left the convent. Baby had no jaundice and mother had no sutures. Luisa's mother stood in the doorway.

"Hermana Catalina, I knitted this alpaca sweater for you. Thank you for the care you gave my daughter and first granddaughter."

I was thrilled to see the beige-and-white sweater. I knew she had hand spun the alpaca wool into fine thread before knitting this sweater. Knowing how much work had gone into this gift made it very special.

I said, "You're very welcome, Señora. Thank you for this lovely sweater."

Luisa gave me the greatest gift. "I'll teach Aymara women and parteras what I've learned from you, Hermana Catalina."

*The dream I had in Northern Perú ten years ago of teaching preventative medicine to parteras is now being fulfilled through Luisa. I feel like I've come full circle. Gracias al Señor.*

It was the eve of the Fiesta de Las Cruces. All Peruvian celebrations start on the eve of the feast day, just as Latin American birthday celebrations start on the eve of the birthday. On May 2nd around 3 p.m., I heard drums beating and flutes playing in the distance. Sister Gloria said, "Come on, Sister Kathleen, the party has begun. Let's join them."

"Sure. Where are they going?"

"The drummers and flute players lead the parade of people carrying the three crosses through the streets then up the highest mountain in Moho. All celebrations, be they weddings, funerals or anniversary feast days take place on this mountain top. Once everyone gathers on the mountain, I'll bless the crosses with holy water. The crosses will then be decorated with garlands and planted in the rocky soil where they'll remain until next year."

Sister Gloria and I were separated in the ebb and flow of the crowd on our ascent. An Aymara woman in a colourful flared skirt and long black braids dangling from beneath her bowler hat grabbed both of my hands and danced me up the mountain to the beat of the drums. Her firm grip made me feel secure. She pulled me along, stomping in circles. The step was similar to the polka step. Everyone was dancing, even men carrying tables upside-down on their heads danced. She was turning me constantly, but on one turn, I saw Lake Titicaca. *What a pivotal moment. I'm dancing above Lake Titicaca. This is the closest to Heaven I've ever been. It's better than being in an airplane.*

On the mountain top Sister Gloria stood amidst the crowd. "With this holy water I bless these three crosses in remembrance of the three crosses on Mount Golgotha where Jesus was victorious over death. With Him we live victoriously."

Everyone responded, "Alleluia."

The drummers and flute players raised a toast from tin cups of chicha, a potent drink made from fermented corn. The cups circulated in the crowd for each person to raise a toast. When I received a cup, I did what I saw everyone else do. I tilted the cup to spill a little, to give Pacha Mama, Mother Earth, a drink to ensure a good harvest. I gave Pacha Mama a hearty drink of chicha, then wet my lips before passing the cup forward to be topped up again!

Chapter Forty-Five

## HEIGHTENED VIGILANCE

The increase in numbers and activities of Shining Path in the mid-eighties dominated and terrorized Perú. My Peruvian friend who taught crafts and pottery in a Lima prison told me, "Cati, there are a lot of Shining Path prisoners here in the Lurigancho prison. They are highly motivated and disciplined individuals. Their prison cells are clean. They do push-ups several times a day. Their slogan, 'The People's War' is on their cell walls."

"I hear that they're brutal and kill innocent people at close range," I said.

"Yes, this is true. But when they go into a mountain village to kill, they only kill who they were sent in to kill. Whereas the military and the Sinchis, go to the same village and massacre everyone: men, women, children and babies. They say, 'If a person has been in contact with Shining Path, the person is a future terrorist'; that is their justification for genocide."

Sinchis is the Quechua nickname for the National Police of Perú (PNP). Once in Lima I saw them close up. I couldn't breathe or move from where my feet were planted in the crowd. There

*Father Bob Dolan SJ (R.I.P.) with orphaned children in Huancayo where the Sendero Luminoso (Shining Path) had killed their parents.*

was something about them in their red angular berettas that provoked a deep fear in me.

Now as I listened to my friend's praise of the Shining Path prisoners I was disturbed. *She sounds like a sympathizer.*

She read my face and said, "Cati, I'm not saying I support violence by either side. I'm saying the massacres we're reading about daily in the newspapers aren't done by the terrorist group. They are done by the anti-terrorists and the anti-narcotics PNP division of the Guardia de Civil and the military. Just like last week's massacre of the Shining Path prisoners."

"What are you talking about?"

"Don't you know about this massacre, Cati?"

"I only arrived here, in Lima, yesterday. I left Moho last week and didn't have access to radio."

"The military stormed three prisons in Lima, killing 240 prisoners."

I was too horrified to say anything. I made the sign of the cross.

After a moment I said, "This sounds like the December 14, 1983 attack on Lurigancho prison. Do you remember? Sister Joan Sawyer, from Ireland, was killed along with the prisoners."

"Yes, I remember it alright. Sister Joan and I worked together in Lurigancho. I was fortunate not to be there that infamous day." Her worried expression deepened her wrinkles. "Cati, Perú is in a very dangerous political situation. No one is safe. We are at war. Shining Path on one side and the military and Sinchis on the other. This won't end until the leader, Abimael Guzman, is caught."

"Are you going to continue working in the Lurigancho prison?"

"No, not for the time being. I'm too shaken up to help anyone."

"I'm feeling the same right now."

This was the general reaction to the massacres, an emotional paralysis. A sense of not knowing what to do, what to think, who to trust, how to live. I personally felt numb. Afraid yet determined not to run home to safety.

※ ※ ※

On my next trip to Lima, I sat by the window in the middle of the long-distance bus. Every seat was occupied. I was the only gringa.

During the night the bus stopped at a checkpoint in the desert. A civil guard in his early thirties boarded the bus. He looked at the driver's passenger list, and shouted from the front, "Foreigner, get off the bus."

I whispered to the Peruvian woman whose shoulder leaned against mine, "Start talking to me." I held her gaze.

She whispered back, "The civil guard wants you to get off the bus and go into his office."

"I know. But let's pretend we're deep in conversation and don't know he's talking to me."

The civil guard yelled for the second time, "Foreigner, get off the bus."

The silent atmosphere spoke of tension. I continued to hold the woman's gaze and she mine. Then it happened.

The civil guard came down the aisle and stopped at our row. Peering at me, he said, "You're a foreigner. Get off the bus."

In an innocent voice, I said, "Who ME?"

"Yes, YOU."

"I'm Peruvian."

"Give me your passport."

I slowly bent forward to reach for my carry-on bag at my feet. With passport in hand, I said in a passionate Spanish voice, "I'm more Peruvian than you are. You are Peruvian because your birth certificate says you are. I'm Peruvian because my heart is Peruvian. I choose to live here."

I handed him my passport.

He handed it back to me. Then he removed his hard-brimmed uniform hat, bowed to me, and said, "Bien dicho," (Well said) and left the bus. When the bus pulled away from the checkpoint back onto the highway, the passengers applauded. I felt cold, tired and shaky, but grateful I had avoided the possibility of being raped and killed had I gotten off the bus.

※ ※ ※

A FEW YEARS LATER ON November 16, 1989, came the devastating news that two Jesuits – four men and two women – had been killed in San Salvador. This atrocity profoundly affected every member of our team. I remember how we embraced in tears. I remember the people from the three pueblos jovenes bringing flowers and sharing our grief.

A month later the Peruvian bishops warned all religious men and women, "Be vigilant and pray for peace."

Did the killing of the Jesuits in San Salvador motivate Shining Path to start their dessert? On September 27, 1990, Shining Path killed Sister Agustina Rivas Lopez, nicknamed Sister Aguchita, a Peruvian sister in her early sixties who preached peace in the Amazon jungle where drug trafficking flourished. She was taken at gunpoint to the plaza and shot in the head along with six villagers.

The sad fact is that it took the killing of the Australian sister, Irene McCormack, in Huasahuasi, on May 21, 1991, to draw world-wide attention to a decade of terrorism in Perú. While I was no longer in Perú when Sister Aguchita and Sister Irene were brutally killed, I received news of these happenings within hours.

Recently, I interviewed Sister Maureen by phone and this is what she shared.

"The killing of Sister Irene was a huge blow to our community. Sister Jenny, our Australian sister, Sister Mary Lynn, and I were personal friends of both Sister Irene and Sister Dorothy. Sister Jenny and Sister Mary Lynn went to the funeral but I couldn't. After the funeral we stayed with Sister Dorothy who worked with Sister Irene in Huasahuasi (in the Peruvian Andes) but was in Lima when the killing occurred. Sister Dorothy knew that she was the target and felt horrible that Sister Irene was taken instead.

Similar to Sister Aguchita, Sister Irene was shot in the head in the plaza along with four villagers. Shining Path's style of execution."

We were lost in our own reflections for a while. Then I dared to ask, "Maureen, how was it for you in the time between my leaving Perú in February 1990 and you leaving in October 1992?"

"Sister Mary Lynn and I were asked to accompany our four postulants to Lima for on-going spiritual training. We rented a warehouse type of building with no electricity. It was near the parish church. The locals were too afraid of the Shining Path to rent to us. This pueblo joven was blocks from Lurigancho prison and became Shining Path's stronghold in Lima. Their goal was to take over Lima. They did this by indoctrinating the youth and threatening to kill them if they didn't join them. Sister Mary Lynn and I feared for our young postulants."

"No kidding."

Sister Maureen continued, "A youth said to me, 'Jesus was like the terrorists. He fought for the poor and the terrorists fight for the poor.' I told him, 'No, Jesus isn't like the terrorists. Terrorists kill. Jesus didn't kill anyone.'

"That night we were woken shortly after midnight with loud heavy banging on the warehouse metal door. Sister Mary Lynn was calm in the pitch blackness but I was trembling so badly my teeth were clattering. Eventually the banging stopped. There were no windows in this warehouse which allowed us to light candles and pray Psalm 91. These lines comforted us:

*You need not fear the terrors of the night,*
*nor the arrows that fly in the daytime.*
*No disaster can overtake you, or plague*
*come near your tent.*
*You yourself will remain unscathed, I am*
*with you in trouble.*

"Kathleen, my anxiety attacks were so severe that Sister Mary

Lynn and I discerned we needed to move to a safer part of Lima. Not long after we moved, we heard on the radio that Abimael Guzman had been captured. It was September 12, 1992. Our relief was tremendous. In Lima and every Peruvian city, people danced in the streets. I rejoiced but was too traumatized to remain in Perú. I returned to Canada a few weeks later."

I thanked Sister Maureen for sharing her petrifying story. Then I said to her, "It's taken us thirty years after Guzman's captivity and now his recent death on Sept. 11, 2021, to share how terrorism affected us."

"Yes, and how timely it is that your book coincides with his death. The closure of an epic journey."

## Chapter Forty-Six

## FAREWELL

Virginia was sewing when I arrived on Sunday afternoon for a short visit. "Edith, make your godmother a cup of camomile tea," she told her eight-year-old daughter.

Peruvian children have many godmothers. A godmother for baptism, for first holy communion, for confirmation, for school activities, and for graduation. The role of the godmother is twofold: to provide moral guidance to the godchild and to give financial support to the parents. When Virginia asked me to be Edith's godmother for her first holy communion, she assured me, "Hermana Catalina, Edith is having two godmothers for this occasion. You'll be her spiritual guide and her second godmother will be her financial supporter. Would you accept to be Edith's godmother?"

"Yes, I accept. It's an honour to be asked. Thank you."

From where I was seated, I could observe both Edith preparing the tea and Virginia sewing Edith's first communion dress. Edith dipped a ladle into a bucket of cold water. The aluminum bucket sat on the uneven concrete kitchen floor. She put the ladle of water in a pot, lit the kerosene stove, heated the water, and poured it over the tea. *Oh Lord, protect me. I'm about to drink crude un-boiled water.*

I shuddered, but not wanting to get Edith in trouble I said, "Thank you, Edith."

I drank the tea and said, "That was a delicious cup of tea."

Eight weeks later I was diagnosed with paratyphoid fever and parasites. It was the first time I had been seriously ill after 20 years in South America. Sister Maureen was on home leave which meant Sister Mary Lynn became my sole provider.

"Kathleen, I'm happy to make dietary meals, clean your room, and spend time with you but this is on condition you remain in bed. No more getting up to the outhouse, or leaving your bed for any reason, not even to go to chapel. You need to preserve energy. Are we in agreement?"

"Yes. Thank you, Mary Lynn. I'll be a good patient from now on."

I experienced the classical symptoms of paratyphoid fever: the gradual onset of fever and frontal headache, like a smack over the eyes, in late afternoon and night. In the mornings and early afternoons, I felt like a fake sitting in bed waiting for breakfast and lunch to be served to me. My diet was very bland. Boiled chicken, potatoes, rice and veggies. No red meat. No raw fruit. No salad. I was allowed fish or chicken as long as neither was fried. Jello came with every meal.

After weeks of this diet, Sister Mary Lynn said, "Kathleen, I have a treat for you."

She handed me a large tin of peaches. "You deserve this as you've been such a good patient."

My immediate reaction was guilt. We sisters tried to live poverty as the people around us were forced to live it even though we had money. We never bought in bulk or food we considered a luxury. A tin of peaches was definitely a luxury!

"Thank you, Mary Lynn. I'll savour them and make them last."

I ate two thin slices twice a day. Sadly, by day four the remaining peaches spoiled in the small kerosene fridge. I learned that day to live and enjoy what I have in the present and not to plan for the future.

The first emotional struggle I had to deal with was anger. My mind knew there was work I had to do. People relied on me. At that time, I had never heard of Rene Descartes and his mind-body separation theory. But this is exactly what I experienced. *How come my body won't listen to me? Why is my body betraying me?* In the long days and nights alone, I was forced to confront the angers I hadn't known I had until my body conked out. Sickness was the beginning of a deep healing process. I began to treasure contemplation, a state of being, versus my former state of doing.

After two months the fever and headaches, as well as the rotten-egg tasting burps, caused by the parasites, stopped. I thought I was better.

Sister Mary Lynn agreed, "Yes, Kathleen, I think you could start to be mobile again."

I wasn't out of bed three days when I had a relapse.

Late one afternoon, sick with fever, chills and a blinding frontal headache, I became consciously aware of St. Ignatius of Loyola's words: "I don't ask to be poor or rich, to be healthy or unhealthy, to be loved or unloved." And with deep joy I knew for the first time in my life this was true for me. I didn't have to be healthy. I didn't have to be rushing around doing things. I was everything I needed to be in this physical unhealthy state.

Little did I know the Lord was preparing me to let go of everything I was attached to emotionally and even spiritually. I no sooner was fully recovered when I received a letter from my sister, Bonnie. The first line of her letter read, "I'm sorry to tell you, Mum is no better."

Tears immediately streamed down my face. I didn't read further. I went to Sister Maureen, who had returned from her home leave, and to Sister Mary Lynn. "My mother is ill." Now I was weeping inconsolably.

"Kathleen," Sister Maureen said. "I'll go with you to the Immigration Office. You're going to need a salida [permit] to leave the country."

In the immigration office a stocky officer sat at his wide shiny glass-covered wooden desk. "How may I help you, Sisters?"

"Sister Kathleen is going to fly from Lima tonight and needs a salida," Sister Maureen said.

"You know you are supposed to apply for a salida weeks before you're scheduled to leave the country." He was really annoyed. "I'm tired of foreigners thinking they're privileged people and can demand a salida on the spot."

I had been dry-eyed when I entered his office, but his harsh voice provoked tears as I blurted out, "If your people didn't steal our mail, I'd have known my mother was ill a long time ago. I found out today that my mother is very ill in Canada."

He changed from the lion on the attack to the lion protector. He picked up his phone. "I need you to have a salida at Jorge Chavez airport made out for Sister Kathleen Ann Kelly for her flight to Montreal tonight."

When he hung up the phone, he said in a fatherly tone, "I hope your mother will recover, Sister Kathleen. I'm sorry your mail was stolen. It's an on-going problem for the government. I wish you all the best. And thank you for your dedication to my people."

Sisters Maureen, Mary Lynn and I boarded the plane to Lima. There, we had time to eat and take a nap before they accompanied me to the airport at midnight. My sudden exit from Perú left me with no opportunity for any farewell to my Peruvian friends and family.

Once I returned to Canada the impact of living under violence for a decade haunted me. I had repeated nightmares but shared this with no one. A repeated dream was that I was back in Perú surrounded by terrorists. I'd say to myself in the dream, "Why did you return to this violence when you were safe in Canada?" I'd wake in a sweat. I had no knowledge of Post-Traumatic Stress Syndrome in 1990. Nor was I offered any re-entry cultural help. The irony was that I was a foreigner in Perú but felt completely at home. In my home country I felt a foreigner and not at home.

※ ※ ※

I LEFT RELIGIOUS LIFE IN May 1991 but remain an advocate for social justice and human rights. I feel I entered religious life at the best time and left at the best time. In gratitude for my life, I share these memories with you. I hope my book will help us, as world pilgrims, to be compassionate and tolerant with refugees trying to make a home in a foreign country.

## ACKNOWLEDGEMENTS

BANNER, CHRIS
Thanks, Chris, for introducing me to the MS Word program. It saved me time and the environment paper!

BATCHELOR, BRUCE
A debt of gratitude to you, Bruce, for accepting to publish my manuscript after fifteen literary agencies didn't respond to my submissions. It's truly an honor to have someone of your calibre in the publishing and marketing world hold my manuscript with such care.

BATCHELOR, MARSHA
How I appreciate your creative spirit. Your abstract paintings and hand-designed carpets touch my heart. You are indeed a gift of joy in our crazy world. Thank you, Marsha, tremendously for capturing the essence of my book in your cover design. And for the effective formatting of this book.

DEANGELIS, MARJORIE
To you, my dear novitiate companion of 60 years, I thank you for praying that I'd find the perfect publisher for my memoir. Your prayers were indeed answered favourably! Marjorie has recently self-published Cameos of Kenya.

FLANNERY, LYNDA
My dear faithful friend and proofreader. Thanks, Lynda, for your continued constructive criticisms and encouragement. Your support has meant a lot to me. Thanks for reading and re-reading the latest version of the same story!

### IMDEKE, BRENDA (SISTER)
Am very grateful to you for finding these photos of my mother's profession day in the archives and mailing them to me. I remember photos were taken but had never seen them. Naturally, after all these years, I treasure them. Thank you for mailing them to me.

### KENYON, MICHAEL
What a blessing to have had you, Michael, for my editor. We shared an intuitively akin spirit from the get-go. You always understood what I was trying to say even when what I wrote was in a mumble-jumble. Thanks so much for the countless hours of editing and for appreciating my missionary background.

### LAFFERTY, KATHLEEN
My detailed proofreader. Thank you, Kathleen, for your sharp eye in dissecting unfamiliar vocabulary. You challenged me to elaborate on how a historical event impacted my life when you were unaffected by the same event. You taught me to bridge generational gaps by explaining.

### LIBRARIANS OF CHEMAINUS AND THE COMOX VALLEY
Thank you for your persistent research in obtaining the required 1983 *Reader's Digest* article for me. Each one of you were so pleasant and helpful.

### MAYSE, SUSAN
This is the wise woman who strongly encouraged me to write a memoir instead of writing a novel with myself as the central character. Susan is an award-winning writer and a seasoned editor. Thank you, Susan, for believing in me and for guiding me on how to get started.

### MISS JENNY
My emotional spiritual compass! Her purrs and snuggles comforted me when words on paper didn't come easy. Or she'd make me laugh with her high-tailing it when I was on a run. Thank you, Jenny, for growing older with me.

MOORE, ANNE (SISTER)
Thank you for sending me the photo of Broughton Hall to place in my memoir and providing me with the year that Broughton Hall was sold.

MORTON, KATE
Thank you for not accepting to be a ghostwriter for me in 2020. You told me, "I can tell by the way you write an email you're quite capable of writing your own story. Now, do it!" Thanks, Kate, for pushing me in this endeavour. Kate Morton is an acclaimed Australian novelist.

O'DONNELL, EILEEN (NÉE HEALY)
My dear County Cork friend with whom I've shared a nursing career and religious life, I thank you for loving the way I write a story. I guess we're both leprechaun storytellers!

ORBAN, PATRICIA (SISTER)
Only you, Patricia, know how instrumental you've been in helping me share these Peruvian stories. You encouraged me to be vulnerable in reliving the traumatic memories and joyful when reliving the nostalgic cultural memories. Thank you for letting me read you a bedtime story when I needed a listening ear.

OTHER PERSONNEL
To family members, friends and acquaintances who have faithfully accompanied me in these two and a half years of writing. As a few of you said, "I want to be the first to hold your published book in my hands." Thanks for your patience and sharing this journey with me.

PERUVIAN SOULMATES
Thank you for loving me and allowing me to experience your rich cultural values that have shaped my life. Muchisimos gracias.

> "To the right, books…
> to the left, a teacup.
> In front of me, the fireplace…
> There's no greater happiness than this."
>
> —*Taiga*

Manufactured by Amazon.ca
Bolton, ON

34780230R00160